LISTEN TO LISTS   Edited by Lina Brion and Detlef Diederichsen, with contributions by Kristoffer Cornils, Maria Eriksson, Jasmine Guffond, Liz Pelly, and Robert Prey

Listen to Lists

Edited by
Lina Brion and Detlef Diederichsen

Contents

Die 20 Gewinner in deutscher Sprache

Die 20 internationalen Gewinner

Hits DER WOCHE
BRAVO-DISCO 3

1 So bist du
Peter Maffay

1 We don't talk anymore
Cliff Richard

3 Frei und abgebrannt
Bernhard Brink

Jürgen holt mächtig auf

Bernhard immer stärker

1		1 So bist du — Peter Maffay	1		1 We don't talk anymore — Cliff Richard	
2		2 Nachts, wenn alles schläft — Howard Carpendale	2		2 Gimme, gimme, gimme — Abba	
3		3 Frei und abgebrannt — Bernhard Brink	3		3 A Walk in the Park — Nick Straker Band	
4	4	Du hattest keine Tränen mehr — Peter Maffay	4	5	I was made for loving you — Kiss	
5	9	Du wirst auch ohne mich leben — Jürgen Drews	5	4	1–2–3–4 Red Light — Teens	
6	6	Schachmatt — Roland Kaiser	6	9	Video killed the Radio Star — Buggles	
7	5	Schulschluß — Jürgen Drews	7	6	Whatever you want — Status Quo	
8	7	El Lute — Michael Holm	8	7	Baby it's up to you — Smokie	
9	8	Ich liebe dich — Peter Orloff	9	8	Boy oh Boy — Racey	
10	11	Ich werde geh'n heute nacht — Mary Roos	10	16	Crazy little Thing called Love — Queen	
11	13	Ich steh' auf Rock'n'Roll — Jürgen Drews	11	10	I don't like Mondays — Boomtown Rats	
12	10	Wie du — Paola	12	11	Voulez vous — Abba	
13	18	Ich wär' so gern wie du — Bernhard Brink	13	13	She's in Love with you — Suzi Quatro	
14	14	Das Lied von Manuel — Manuel & Pony	14	17	Maybe — Thom Pace	
15	15	Wenn ich geh' — Wolfgang Petry	15	12	Don't bring me down — Electric Light Orchestra	
16	16	Moskau — Dschingis Khan	16	14	El Lute — Boney M.	
17	19	Ich denk' oft an Marianne — Waterloo & Robinson	17	NEU!	When you're in Love — Dr. Hook	
18	17	Bleib am Ball — Boy	18	20	Tusk — Fleetwood Mac	
19	12	Der Verräter — Dschingis Khan	19	19	I want you to want me — Cheap Trick	
20	20	Nicht zu fassen — Ingrid Peters	20	NEU!	Message in a Bottle — Police	

Queen hauen auf den Putz

Police greifn ein

Englands Top-Hits
1 (1) ANOTHER BRICK IN THE WALL Pink Floyd
2 (–) I HAVE A DREAM Abba
3 (2) WALKING ON THE MOON Police
4 (–) DAY TRIP TO BANGOR Fiddler's Dream
5 (4) I ONLY WANT TO BE WITH YOU Tourists
6 (–) RAPPERS DELIGHT Sugarhill Gang
7 (–) WONDERFUL CHRISTMAS Paul McCartney
8 (6) QUE SERA MI VIDA Gibson Brothers
9 (10) MY SIMPLE HEART Three Degrees
10 (–) BRASS IN POCKET Pretenders

Songs, die auf dem Weg in die Top-Twenty sind
Hadschi Halef Omar — Dschingis Khan
Sie ist kalt — Marianne Rosenberg
Früh-Stück — Gebrüder Blattschuß
Wie frei willst du sein — Howard Carpendale

Union City Blue — Blondie
Such a Night — Racey
Oowatanite — Clout
Take the long Way home — Supertramp

Amerikas Top-Hits
1 (2) ESCAPE Rupert Holmes
2 (1) NO MORE TEARS Streisand & Summer
3 (3) PLEASE DON'T GO K. C. & Sunshine Band
4 (6) SEND ONE YOUR LOVE Stevie Wonder
5 (5) LADIES NIGHT Kool & The Gang
6 (4) BABE Styx
7 (9) JANE Jefferson Starship
8 (10) WE DON'T TALK ANYMORE Cliff Richard
9 (–) DO THAT TO ME . . . Captain & Tennille
10 (–) ROCK WITH YOU Michael Jackson

Jede Woche verschickt BRAVO 3000 Stimmkarten an Leser, die sich an BRAVO-Aktionen beteiligt haben, und fragt nach Euren Lieblings-Songs. Eure Antworten ergeben die 20 Top-Hits in deutscher Sprache und die 20 fremdsprachigen Spitzen-Schlager in Deutschland. – Die englische und die amerikanische Hitliste basieren auf Fachzeitschriften aus Großbritannien und den USA.

Introduction
The Order of Playlists

For some time now, lists have been creating order in the world of music. With the emergence of mass media in the mid-twentieth century, the charts ("hit lists") were established for the first time and then increasingly differentiated according to genres and formats. Soon these rankings were adapted by radio stations whose countdowns from number ten to the top spot managed to give music presentation an exciting dramaturgy. From the 1960s and '70s onwards, shows like the BBC's *Top of the Pops* in the UK or the ZDF *Hitparade* in Germany created a telegenic stage for the list format. At the same time, new lists appeared in the radio landscape: "Playlists" were designed to put an end to the omnipotence of radio disc jockeys who hosted and compiled their own programs—at the service of the new goal of a "homogeneous listening experience." In the 1980s, under pressure from commercial radio broadcasters, even the last bastions of public broadcasting surrendered to this predominant principle, allowing music editors and then increasingly algorithms to define playlists, whose main purpose was to make it difficult for listeners to switch to another station. Radio DJs regressed into jovial chatterboxes with no authority over content, while DJs with selection and curation skills in the various dance music genres found new fields of activity in clubs and at raves. The genuine or purported music experts, meanwhile, redirected their compliance with the list format to magazines with their year-end rankings, or to large-scale displays such as "The 500 Best Guitar Solos of All Time."

Yet the list format experienced its greatest triumph with the advent of music streaming in the 2010s. The streaming playlist is one of the latest variations of the popular practice of enumerating, classifying and cataloguing, selecting and sequencing. Not only has it replaced the primary formats of music consumption (buying vinyl records, burning audio tapes or CDs), but people today instead activate their access to digital audio libraries by accepting the unread Terms of Service. It also embodies the new economic model of digital platform capitalism. Streaming services play a central role in the tendency to convert all areas of life into computerized data and to exploit them as such. Here the traded commodity is less the music file than the information about the users' listening behavior. The playlist serves as an interface that intertwines access to music with the collection of music-consumer data.

As classification systems, playlists contextualize music files according to predefined categories of mood and activity. This form of compiling individual tracks—whether algorithmically personalized or editorially "recommended"—not only influences listeninWg behavior and musical aesthetics, but increasingly also the way musical sound structures everyday life and spaces. The business model of ad-based services requires a media format that continuously generates personalized records of consumer activity and mood in real time: "soundtrack every moment of your life." The result is neo-Muzak, the industrial functionalization of music as environment, stimulation substance, and self-regulation technology.

This volume explores what makes the playlist so well suited as a sorting and recommendation format for organizing data production. In what way does it serve as an ordering, logistical, and communicative instrument? Which scientific methods and representation models are embedded in the playlist format? And what role does listening play as, on the one hand, an activity and a sensual perception, and as a monitoring "listening-in" technique, on the other?

Together with a Swedish research team and the tools of reverse engineering, media scientist Maria Eriksson has taken apart the streaming service Spotify to uncover its inner workings. The artist Jasmine Guffond also uses data analysis for a similar investigative approach: A browser extension converts Internet cookies into sound, enabling users to turn the tables, and listen-in to the tracking of their online activities. For this volume, the two authors have interviewed each other.

Kristoffer Cornils situates the playlist in a cultural history of the list, delineating its role in the political economy of music. Robert Prey investigates the format of the programmed flow and the behaviorist assumptions about the music-listening subject, both crucial foundations for the datafication of music. Liz Pelly's polemic against the logic of the playlist, which combines principles of advertising and exploitation and leads to passivity and the homogenization of music, argues for an alternative practice of conscious listening that ultimately leaves the order of the playlist behind.

Lina Brion and Detlef Diederichsen

Translated from the German by Kevin Kennedy

Disassemble to Understand

Jasmine Guffond: Your research team examined the economic and business history of Spotify from its beginnings as a start-up to its 2018 IPO (initial public offering). These kinds of economic histories tend to be underemphasized in cultural studies; can you elaborate on the importance of "financialization as a structuring principle of media history"?[1]

> Maria Eriksson: In *Spotify Teardown*, we attempted to apply that well-established principle of "following the money" to understand Spotify's growth and current role within the music industries. By looking at the history of Spotify and carefully tracing how the influx of capital has changed the company over time, we set out to answer questions such as: What kind of autonomy does Spotify possess as a corporate enterprise? and How has Spotify's business model and ways of presenting itself transformed in relation to its need to attract external funding?
>
> In our attempt to answer these questions, we mapped Spotify's business structure (including its ownership organization and offshore tax-planning arrangements) as well as the network of investors and venture capital firms (including major record labels and actors like Goldman Sachs, the Coca-Cola Company, and the Russian investment fund Digital Sky Technologies) who have helped sustain and magnify the "hype" around Spotify throughout its history. What we found was that disclosing such economic transactions can work as an effective tool for dispelling the progressive and alternative aura that many start-up companies work hard to maintain. At its core, Spotify is no different from other highly speculative and profit-driven online businesses, and our strategy of exploring its financialization helped reveal just that.

JG: Your research team also employed a methodology of bot-driven research as an interventionist technique. How does this relate to the idea of Spotify Teardown?

1   Maria Eriksson, Rasmus Fleischer, Anna Johansson, et al., *Spotify Teardown: Inside the Black Box of Streaming Music*. Cambridge and London: MIT Press, 2019, p. 35.

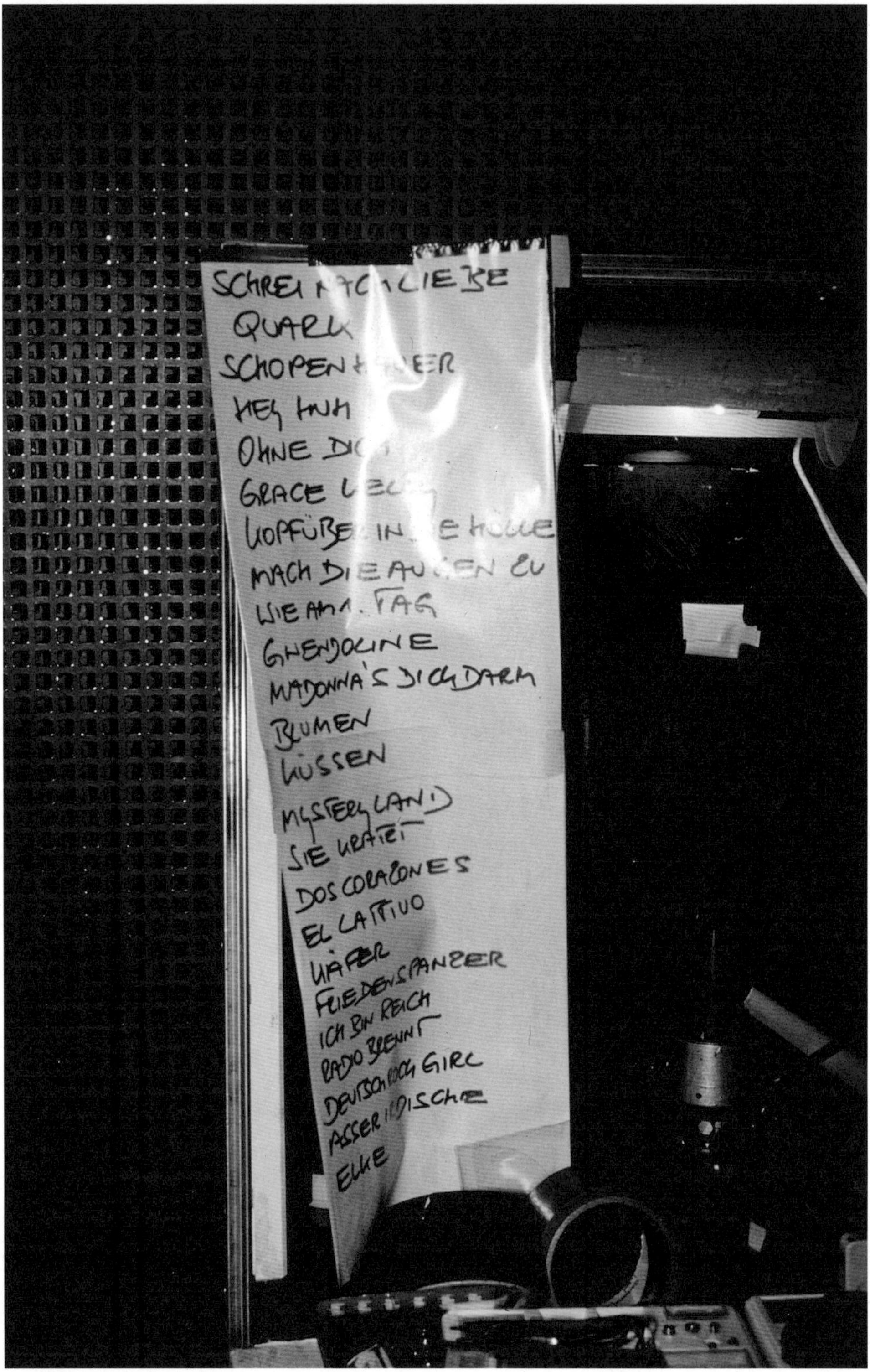
QUARK
GWENDOLINE
BLUMEN
MYSTERY LAND
DOS CORAZONES
FRIEDENSPANZER
ICH BIN REICH
RADIO BRENNT
ELKE

ME: A main idea within our research group was to find a way of not just studying Spotify from a distance, but also actively *engage* and set things in motion within the platform in order to study its dynamics. Our use of bots (or software scripts that were programmed to imitate Spotify users to study the platform's music recommendation system) was one such method. Creating a record label for research purposes and engaging in speculative software design to interrogate the phenomenon of ad blocking on Spotify were two other methods. *Spotify Teardown* is very much built around these interventions, seeking to actively test, probe, and explore how Spotify works at both a practical and theoretical level. Maybe one could say that this approach shares some similarities with your artistic practice, in the sense that we all seem to share an interest in tinkering with the operations of technological systems—for example, by backtracking their outputs and searching for openings that could allow us to discern what is happening within them.

In the *Spotify Teardown* book we also borrow the notion of "teardown" from reverse engineering processes, where generally the term refers to a process of disassembling technical products and identifying their key components, in order to study their functionality. In a similar way, we wanted to disassemble Spotify and identify its key components and functions—not least in order to problematize how the company is commonly conceptualized and described.

JG: What did your use of bots and automated "fake" user accounts reveal about Spotify's recommended playlists? In the article "Keep Smiling," for example, you write about Spotify's "chrononormative effects."[2] Could you elaborate on what this means?

ME: My colleague Anna Johansson and I explored how the descriptive texts and images that surround Spotify's Featured Playlists help contextualize music and push forward ideas regarding "the good life."[3] Here, we were particularly interested

2   Maria Eriksson and Anna Johansson, "'Keep Smiling!': Time, Functionality and Intimacy in Spotify's Featured Playlists," *Cultural Analysis,* vol.16, no.1 (2017), pp.67–82.
3   Eriksson et al., *Spotify Teardown,* p.35.

in studying differences and similarities in the types of content that Spotify shows to users in different countries. To do this, we created fictional Spotify user accounts that had identical settings, except for one feature: their registered nationality and Internet Protocol (IP) address. We used predesigned scripts and programmed these user accounts (or bots) to automatically perform a series of tasks within the Spotify platform (signing in, pausing for a couple of seconds, and then signing out again). Meanwhile, we carefully documented how Spotify approached the accounts visually, textually, and musically.

We studied in detail how Spotify addressed three fictional user accounts—a Swedish, an Argentinian, and a North American—on an hourly basis, for the duration of a week. Our analysis showed that Spotify's recommendations followed surprisingly similar patterns across the countries studied. All music recommendations were tightly bound to the time of the day and ideas regarding how one should spend one's life (waking up with good vibes and getting ready for work in the morning, making sure to maintain concentration and productivity in the afternoon, relaxing or spending time with friends and family in the evenings, and so on). Building on the work of Elizabeth Freeman,[4] we conceptualized Spotify's way of addressing users as having chrononormative effects—that is, as prescribing normative temporal patternings of social life. Such chrononormative effects, we argue, organize human life towards maximum productivity in ways that align with neoliberal, capitalist—and often heteronormative—ideologies (work hard, stay healthy, maintain productivity, uphold a passionate love life, and improve your mental state, and so on).

JG: Spotify playlists, thematically curated according to moods and daily activities, reduce music to a functionary role with obvious connections to Muzak. However, unlike Muzak, the Spotify playlist design intends to reach beyond the timeframe of the workday and the geolocation of the workplace into every aspect of our waking and sleeping lives. What are the cultural and political implications

---

4   Elizabeth Freeman, *Time Binds: Queer Temporalities, Queer Histories*.
Durham, NC, and London: Duke University Press, 2010.

of the infinite and seamless playlist? By reducing the role of music to a utilitarian one, is the potential for art to question and challenge diminished?

> ME: The more time users spend interacting with digital services and applications, the more opportunities platforms have to analyze and sell their data. I believe that we must understand the sharp focus on prepackaged and seeming endless curated playlists within this wider context. While playlists are often presented as a type of "gift" that caters to the individual desires of users—and which can help them escape the presumably tedious task of having to decide what music to play—playlists are also heavily commercialized products for gaining insights about audience behaviors and for regulating what people listen to. In this sense, playlists are not innocent music packages, but vital commodities within the online music economy.
>
> Does this have the potential to diminish the progressive force of music? To some extent, since music is undoubtedly caught in deeper capitalistic spirals of value extraction. However, if the role of music is reduced to a utilitarian one, this may well trigger a counterreaction that could lead to an increase in music's tendency to question and challenge political issues. Personally, I doubt it will ever fully kill off music's progressive potential, since music's ability to have an impact on the world stretches way beyond its presence in curated playlists (thankfully).

JG: You also describe how Spotify's temporal playlist categorizations serve as a surveillance tactic/technology in the sense that it prepares for behavioral marketing. How does this work? Is this simply continuing a tradition in advertising that attempts to manipulate consumers to buy products, or are we seeing the harnessing of music in new and particularly insidious ways?

> ME: Spotify's playlist recommendations often take on a highly personal and intimate tone, although in fact they are broadcast to a wide range of Spotify users all at the same time. This follows a longer tradition where the mass media has tried to create a sense of friendliness, participation, sympathy, and

HEIKE	A=VP			130	Lick
		38	Verliebt(	131	Kurt - Linden
	·Bünne	39	Itsy 1	132	Sandu-show-Maus
3a	EB	40	M.Lou(H.ho)	133	Henketto Susanne
4a	Ballerina	41	Düsseld.	134	Grünew.
5	S.Broken	42	Frieden	135 a/b Liedsfest. Polka
6	R.Lipp.	43	Capri(H.ho)	136 a/b Kleinigk.-VP
7	Bl.Boot	44	Tulpen	137 LORD-VP
8a/b	B.Sund.	45a	Theke-Husar	138 Get - v.Bal (GEB
9a	1000mal	46a	POL.-M.	139 W.Boot-fu
10	Gefühle	47a	Sauf-M.	140 a/b Schön wostig
11	Dich lb.	48a	Marsch-M.	141 LULSA
12a	Seem.	49a	Walzer-M.	85 B.Moom(Polo)
13a	•S.Dom.	50-Eins.	Samba-M.	86a Silence
14	Belinda	51a	See-M.	87a Ewigk.
15	R.-Rosen	52	Ostsew..	88a Alles-lb.
16a	Bella Ven.	53-Eins.	Nordseek.	89 I have SONNE
17a	Pyräus	54	Rosam.(a.Sä.)	90 Spr.-Lb.(o.Ch,gt.) TWIST
	bku.	55	Horch.	91 Br.Girl W.Weste
19	Ibiza	56	Alle Vögel	92 Schloß
20	Erst willst	57a	So 1 Tag	93 Stern
21a	M.Maria	58	TUSCH	•94 a/b Gr.Wein
22a	Veo	59-Can-street X		95a CARMEN
23a	Hooray	60 Eins.	B.Berge.	96 Wh.Chr.
a/b	7 Fäss./EINS	61a	Clement.	97 Cavalleric
a	Denkst	62	Obladi (Ch.V)	98 In Duc Capella (föthe)
a	Marmor	63-Eins.	J.lb.	99 Merry Christ.
	Hd. z. Hi.	64a/b	Alt-Baum	100 Schlitten
	Holzm.	65	Achy	101a K.Angst- m.Zug.
a/b	Bl.-Nacht	66a	Ring	101c K.Angst- o.Zug.
a/b	Schö-We	67a/b	Top TOP	102a Komm ruf- m.Zug
a/b	Denn-lb.Welt	68	Try	102c Komm ruf- o.Zug
	Kl.Welt	69-Eins.	Rhinst.	103 Feliz Kl.To
	Theater(kz)	70	Y.River	104 White Ch. S.Cla
	1000 kl.Stern.	71	Jam.	105 Weihn.v.Tür
	Sonntags	•72a/b	Even Cow.	106a Alle J.
	Jäger	73	Lookg.	107a Kling
	b/c .. B.hese	74		108a J.Bells/dt.-engl.

belonging among audiences through intimate speech.[5] What is clear in the case of Spotify, however, is the company's direct way of using these personal ways of addressing audiences for advertising purposes. During the period of our research, Spotify offered advertisers the possibility of reaching users according to at least eight different activities and moods that playlists include: workout, party, chill, focus, dinner, kids and family, travel, and romance. In this way, Spotify's Featured Playlists are tightly entangled with behavioral marketing—an advertising strategy aimed at segmenting audiences based on their conduct, emotional states, and personality traits. Ultimately, playlists are calculative devices through which users become known, measured, and saleable. Here, it is not primarily about making people listen to more music, but rather converting user data into audience insights that can be sold to third parties.

JG: By capitalizing on music's ability to be emotionally affecting, do you view the recommended playlists as an emotional/psychological form of control or manipulation?

ME: Yes, but so are all forms of music distribution. I don't believe there was ever a time when human beings could somehow access music in a "pure" and "unmanipulated" way. Music is—and always has been—deeply embedded in cultural norms, ideologies, and systems of power, so it would seem unfair to suggest that Spotify is alone in treating music in manipulative ways. Rather, Spotify continues a long history of using music as a means to influence people's ways of thinking and being.

JG: Could you talk a bit more about how online music platforms influence people's access to and enjoyment of music? What are the implications of platforms standardizing our listening experiences?

5   For example, see Donald Horton and R. Richard Wohl, "Mass Communication and Para-Social Interaction: Observations on Intimacy at a Distance" [1956], *Particip@tions*, vol. 3, no. 1 (2006), https://www.participations.org /volume%203/issue%201/3_01_hortonwohl.htm, accessed October 2; and John Durham Peters, "Broadcasting and Schizophrenia," *Media, Culture & Society*, vol. 32, no. 1 (2010), pp. 123–40.

ME: Online music platforms have extensive abilities to govern how music is promoted, valued, packaged, and sold to customers, but they are definitely not the first actors within the music industries to acquire such a position. Record store chains and multinational music publishing houses have played equally key roles in regulating how music reaches audiences. However, compared to their historical predecessors, online music platforms are in a unique position to monetize music and listening in new ways—especially by exploiting the real-time feedback of data from their users. While a record store to some extent loses control over music as soon as it sells a record, platforms can continue to collect data about audiences and monitor their behavior day after day. More than the actual music in itself, this information is the commodity that online services for music are trading.

JG: With Spotify's recent 2020 acquisitions of highly popular podcasts such as The Ringer ($US 200 million) and The Joe Rogan Experience (boasting millions of plays within a twenty-four-hour period) the aim is to dominate another sphere of cultural production and consumption.[6] When only a few actors dominate online access to a particular cultural paradigm, what are the implications for cultural experience, knowledge, and meaning making?

ME: Spotify has attempted to enter new markets several times. A couple of years ago it seemed like the company would start to distribute audiovisual content, and recent signs have indicated that Spotify might start producing hardware. Many of these ideas will never materialize, however, and I think it is still too soon to say whether Spotify will actually stick to its newly chosen blog path.

Having said that, Spotify's decision to invest in podcasts is interesting. Podcasts are a special case in the sense that they often adopt journalistic qualities (since they reach wide audiences and frequently include powerful stakeholders expressing

6   Alex Hern, "Spotify Podcast Deal could make Joe Rogan World's Highest Paid Broadcaster," *The Guardian* (May 24, 2020), https://www .theguardian.com/media/2020/may/24/spotify-podcast-deal-the-joe -rogan-experience, accessed July 15, 2020.

their views) while not necessarily abiding by traditional journalistic codes of standards and ethics—like fact-checking, protecting sources, and giving voice to contrasting viewpoints on controversial topics. This has led quite often to podcasts being caught up in discussions over fake-news, propaganda, and the deterioration of public debate. By promoting and investing in podcasts, Spotify is facilitating the increased influence of this form of cultural expression. I wonder if this might be good reason to consider whether distributors such as Spotify should be held accountable for the content they distribute like other media publishers—at least to some extent.

JG: I can image that Spotify was not amused by your research.

ME: In fact, they threatened our research group with litigation after the release of *Spotify Teardown*. That made me look deeper into the politics of Terms of Service (ToS) agreements—those endlessly long contracts that users have to accept before signing up for an online service. Spotify attempted to sever our research funding, arguing that our methods (which involved scraping information from the Spotify app, creating fictional accounts, and manipulating plays on the Spotify platform) had damaged the company financially. After we received support from our university and funding body, Spotify stepped down from its threats, but the incident shed light on the legal and ethical status of ToS agreements—and the necessity of safeguarding the freedoms of academics, artists, and journalists to critically interrogate major players in the online economy.

Currently, ToS agreements constitute a fascinating category of documents that exist in a legal gray zone. At their core, they are corporate products formulated without governmental oversight, meaning that companies are free to add all sorts of regulations to them—including those that grant themselves exclusive rights to exploit their users' integrity, while at the same time restricting users' ability to scrutinize what is going on at the level of the platform. For instance, it is very common for ToS agreements to forbid users from saving and making public *any* information from platforms (whether in the form of copied text, images, or sound). Were regulations such as these followed to the letter, however, they would seriously inhibit critical investigation from taking place, since the ability to copy, archive, and make information public is central to both science and journalism. Equally pressing is that were violating ToS agreements considered a felony (as Spotify seemed to suggest when it threatened to sue our research group) then online platforms could own unprecedented power to dictate law. ToS agreements are therefore intriguing documents where law, ethics, and politics converge, and I am very interested in exploring their history and influence.

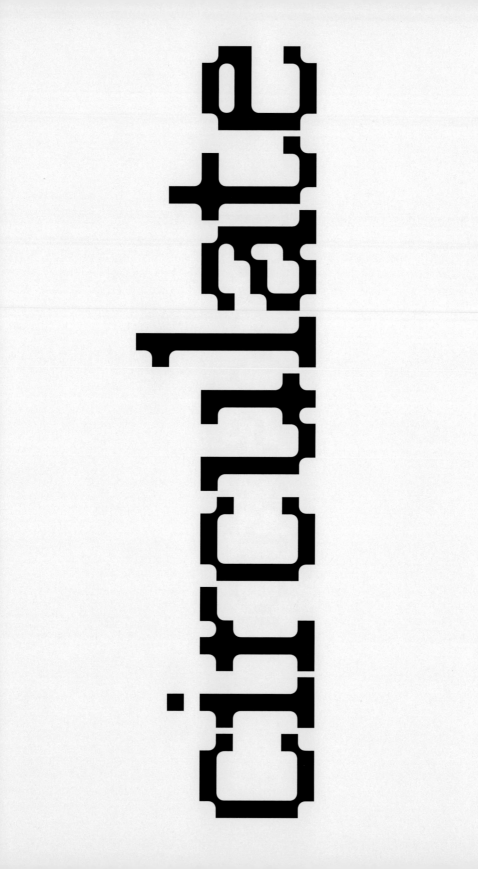

landscape

On the History of the Playlist

The form of the list is the creation of a culture that wants to create order—in communication, knowledge transfer, or in the experience of the world in general. However, the motivation for creating lists can differ as much as the criteria according to which lists are created. As matter-of-fact as any list may appear at first glance, it is always shaped by the interests it implicitly represents. Those who want to create order will either reproduce existing orders, as in *Forbes World's Billionaires List*, or attempt to create new ones, as in the case of electoral lists. This is why each list is not only itself a form of culture, but in turn, forms culture in sociopolitical terms.

The list may be a medium in which what is distinct becomes unified and publicly accessible, but it always starts out from a certain definition of the public sphere, which it helps to construct. What else could a picture listicle such as "50 People You Wish You Knew In Real Life" on the entertainment platform BuzzFeed be other than a normative setting?[1] It assumes a broad congruence of aesthetic-ethical presuppositions while itself determining them. Once written down, lists are always subject to power discourses; they reflect and constitute hierarchies and thus inscribe themselves within cultural processes. What were the Ten Commandments if not a list?

This is also possible in opposition to widely accepted norms. As counterintuitive as it would be, for example, to arrange the Table of Contents of the present book alphabetically according to the titles of the individual contributions, there is no law against it. This is another central feature of the list: It determines its own internal organization and can flout the structure of other lists. Lists are therefore economic in the strict sense of the word—they unite a number of norms under one roof. And they always reflect a supply that either responds to a demand or anticipates it. Every invoice or receipt is, after all, a list of what has been provided or purchased, just as every to-do and shopping list preformulates what is to be provided and purchased. In this way, lists not only sort what is given in the past or present, but also draft instructions for future action. This is why they not only

1   Dave Stopera, "50 People You Wish You Knew In Real Life," *BuzzFeed* (2012, updated January 25, 2019), https://www.buzzfeed.com/daves4/people-you-wish-you-knew-in-real-life#.nvMlX7LBW, accessed July 19, 2020.

constitute a mode of representation for the past and present but also delineate the future.

In pop music, lists have always been used to create systems and orders, construct chronologies, and make knowledge readily accessible for consumption. How else does one obtain an overview of the discography of a hyperactive noise artist like Masami Akita aka Merzbow? In the summer of 2020, the platforms Discogs and Rate Your Music (RYM) listed more than 1,000 and just over 900 recordings respectively that Akita had released as a solo artist or in which he had featured. Although it is unlikely that Akita remembers each and every one of his releases or when and where he first released a particular record, here his complete works are brought into a manageable form with merciless meticulousness.

Yet, beyond this purely archival and cataloguing function, music lists always have an emotional dimension. Mixtapes, playlists? Essentially, these are only lists, but they are much more than the mere sum of their parts. Lists are a form of self-expression and thus reveal something about their creators: quantitative comparisons ("the size of my record collection versus the size of yours") or qualitative judgements ("these are my ten albums for a desert island"), to construct hierarchies ("the ten most anticipated albums of the summer") or solidify them ("the fifty best albums of the 80's").

Music lists provide overviews, thereby facilitating communication about a constantly changing cultural field. In doing so however, they homogenize the heterogeneous, and the spirit of order they communicate in fact clearly contradicts our understanding of music as an art form. If every piece of music dear to us is as unique as we tend to believe, then why is it so easy to convert it into cold, naked numbers along with others of its kind? Because lists are also shaped by harsh economic realities. Charts, for example, derive their legitimacy from presenting changes in constant reference to one another. This is based on the assumption that the audience care about the popularity of a particular song or hold out hope that every ranking will be understood as a recommendation where what is popular will become even more popular. Without lists, there is no pop.

That is why music lists document and enumerate much more than mere facts or personal preferences. Cultural events and associated social movements, technological developments, economic fluctuations—all are gleanable from a comparative look at a few lists.

Thanks to a successful Freddie Mercury biopic, "Bohemian Rhapsody" re-enters the charts in 2018 after decades of absence, and N.W.A.'s "Fuck tha Police" conquers the charts of the streaming world in the summer of 2020 at the same moment that the Black Lives Matter movement takes to the streets to protest against police violence. Both of these examples demonstrate that lists reflect the zeitgeist—whether just a newly kindled collective enthusiasm for pompous prog rock or sociopolitical frustration that erupts into a piece of music. Music lists are always also psychograms, of individuals as well as of whole cultures and societies.

Just as the zeitgeist can change, the form of the list has always changed and continues to do so. This is because its character depends on technological conditions: What is initially transmitted orally, in the form of a canon, is soon etched in print and therefore seems unchangeable, at least until lists become digital and thus modifiable at any time. They are not only documents but also catalysts of cultural upheavals in their own right.

In the twenty-first century, the playlist has become the ubiquitous form of the list of tracks, increasingly preferred to classic formats such as the album, the EP, or the single. Like the physical recording media before it, it has not only changed the way we make music but also the way we perceive it. It is dynamic, personalized, varies from week to week and from user to user, and, as its name suggests, is defined by its playability. It is not merely a document, but also a medium. And just as media shape music, lists shape culture as a whole.

The LP's running time of just under three-quarters of an hour, for instance, triggered a specific conception of the album as a coherent narrative. With the playlist, however, consumers can be creative or even become curators in their own right, rearranging pieces of music according to their own preferences, taking songs out of their contexts and inserting them into new ones. Yet this is not only true for consumers, but also for companies, streaming platforms, with their playlist editors, and, of course, for musicians themselves.

For example, following the initial release of his album *The Life of Pablo* in 2016, Kanye West repeatedly changed its tracklist or replaced the existing tracks with different versions. Thus, the playlist as a type of music list, as a medium-for-itself, and as a field of tension reflects and provokes extensive changes in the reception and production of music—in which personal preferences (my favorite Kanye songs) compete with artistic decisions (Kanye's favorite Kanye songs) as well as the interests of the music industry (the Kanye songs considered most valuable by the respective streaming services)—reflects and provokes extensive changes in the reception and production of music. How could this have come about in the first place?

Music lists can be traced back to the repertoires of traveling musicians, for example, as well as to the hymn boards in Christian worship and practices and even further back than those. These early forms are only literally playlists *avant la lettre*, because playlisting as a cultural technique only begins with the printing press, along with the practice of archiving and cataloguing in list form. From the sixteenth century onwards, collections of scores were printed and sold for the first time and became actively playable as early as the eighteenth and nineteenth centuries. The barrel organ, the pianola, as well as the jukebox are, to varying degrees, based on the automated playback of preselected music, providing the audience with more opportunities for self-expression. Whether in salon or saloon culture, you no longer have to invite a string quartet into your home to show off your taste. The right device with the right selection of musical pieces will do the trick.

The right choice of music—what is the meaning of that exactly? Initially, this is determined by the publishers and then, increasingly from the beginning of the twentieth century, by the bare numbers. The more music becomes available as a commodity, the more important its selection and evaluation is. When US magazine *Variety* prints the very first music charts, it does not rank them. Yet, with the introduction of the singles chart by British magazine *New Musical Express*, founded in 1952, and the Billboard 100 following three years later, this becomes the new norm. The supposed objective ordering principles give way to presentations of economic facts: charts do not list how many listens actually belong to the piece, but merely enumerate the number of copies sold.

Yet, the more you sell, the more you will sell. Although charts claim to reflect the popularity of certain pieces of music with statistical rigor, they in fact also function according to the logic of the so-called bandwagon effect. This means that popular things usually become more so when recognized and presented as such, which is why charts not only ascertain and communicate what is currently popular, but also define what popularity is.

These charts then began to feed the playlists underpinning radio shows on the newly emerging stations, whose content in turn influenced the charts. A single promoted on a radio station, is picked up by others, bought by the audience, enters the charts, and thus increases its airplay—ad infinitum, or at least ad nauseam. Only once everyone is sick of a song does it disappear from the radio playlists and charts. Jacques Attali's thesis, according to which the music industry is not devoted to the production of a supply, but rather to the production of demand itself, is evident in these bizarre feedback loops.[2]

The fact that the music industry wanted to actively trigger such effects becomes obvious no later than 1960, when the US passes a law against so-called payola—the systematic bribery of radio DJs and program editors by music labels and their representatives. In its place, the record companies increase their efforts to have their songs featured in the playlists of the radio stations—hardly less shady, but at least (to some extent) legal—which is why promotion as a branch of the music industry is still growing and flourishing. Various forms of "institutionalized payola" are still relevant,[3] but the charts are increasingly less so, at least for an audience that can become active and is involved in shaping what counts as popular and, accordingly, how popularity is defined.

Like the radio, the record, however, is a medium that compels you to mostly passive consumption: You must get up to turn it over and put the needle on the start of the groove you wish to play, but you cannot really do much more than this. A record's list of tracks, just like a radio playlist, is decided by the music industry and thus primarily follows economic logic. Before the album was elevated to an art form, it was no more than a physical listing of individual pieces, assembled less according to artistic than economic aspects. The "Best-of" album, for example, is aimed at the occasional listener, while real fans are lured with previously unreleased bonus material or simply with the convenience of being able to listen to all of their favorite songs in one

2   Cf. Jacques Attali, *Noise: The Political Economy of Music*, trans. Brian
      Massumi. Minneapolis, University of Minnesota Press, 1985, p.103.
3   This is how Fredric Dannen describes it in his chronicle of the US music
      industry from the 1950s onwards. See Fredric Dannen, *Hit Men:*
      Power Brokers and Fast Money Inside the Music Business. New York:
      Vintage, 1991, p.15.

go for maximum added value. It is not until the 1960s that the album begins to assert itself as a monolithic art form, which it is destined to remain for a long time.

The more notably ubiquitous and seemingly relevant the various lists become in the music industry, the more they turn into an audience fetish. Whether the setlists of concerts, which at best have the aura of having "been there," the playlists of important radio shows only half-listened to, or editorially created bestseller lists that draw their capital from the cool knowledge of some pop magazine, nonetheless, these lists both reveal and shape personal musical experience and primarily turn listeners into passive consumers.

Inscribed in every change of media is the promise of democratization, if not empowerment, and the increase of interpretative authority over the order of musical things. Alongside the widespread introduction of the Sony Walkman in 1979, another revolution is taking place. In his essay "The Walkman Effect," Shuhei Hosokawa draws attention to the "devolution" that accompanies it: For him the portable playback device "represents a functional reduction, technological regression."[4] Yet the author ignores the fact that a new cultural technique is rapidly emerging. Individual pieces are recorded off the radio, off records, or off compact discs—created the same year—onto cassette tape and arranged in a certain order, according to thematic aspects or musical-aesthetic parameters, for example. The listeners generate their own compilations and take the results with them wherever they want. The mixtape is not only a self-created list, but it is also a playable playlist.

With the proliferation of the compact disc and later the CD burner or the CD-ROM in the 1990s, this private and personalized form of playlisting intensifies further. The release of the MP3 in 1993 soon changes the distribution and consumption of music on desktop computers. Music becomes dematerialized, downloadable, and the Internet increasingly becomes the medium for the distribution of audio content. Apple's QuickTime multimedia framework and RealAudio Player by RealNetworks provide round-the-clock access to audio files. Audio content becomes available both on demand and live, thus enabling a form of personalization that radio cannot offer. The

---

4   Shuhei Hosokawa, "The Walkman Effect," *Popular Music,* vol. 4 (1984), pp. 165–80, here p. 168.

audience emancipates itself, at least partially, from the latter's play-lists and definitions of popularity. While mixtaping for the Walkman or the home cassette deck was still bound to the physical limitations of the sound carrier, in programs like the media player Winamp, rolled out in 1997, it becomes, in theory at least, infinitely re-combinable. The times of material scarcity are over; a logic of abundance begins to proliferate.

Due to increasing economic pressure, the industry has to react to this technological–cultural paradigm shift. When Liquid Audio starts selling music as audio files in 1996, alternative distribu-tion channels suddenly emerge. In 1999, two years after mp3.com, Napster goes online. Music circulates without regulation between individual users via the peer-to-peer system. Whereas previously, the so-called piracy of music was still bound to physical formats and hence cumbersome, the dematerialization and copyability of music in file format now enables their effortless and unregulated distribu-tion on the Internet. As the consequence of this new sharing econ-omy, record sales collapse.

A ray of hope is provided by Apple's iTunes Store, rolled out in 2003, whose offer is a clear response to changing consumer behavior. Here, you can buy music either in traditional formats, like the album or the EP, or "unbundled," that is, as single song units.[5] Two years earlier, with the introduction of the iPod, the same company had already presented a device whose design was adapted to the new reception form, allowing consumers to organize individual music files in playlists. In his 2005 book *iPod, Therefore I Am*, Dylan Jones rejoices: "I wasn't consuming music so much as curating it, and the iPod had brought out the anorak in me; I was becoming an organiser, an alphabetiser."[6]

Even more than the classic mixtape, the self-curated iPod play-list is dynamic. Yet, just as the Walkman's technological devolution initiates new cultural developments, the new technology does not necessarily trigger cultural progress. Jones continues: "I had my own canon, one built on experiences I had when I was back in my teens, when, if I chose to, I would play an album until I liked it, no matter

5   Alan B. Krueger, *Rockonomics: What the Music Industry Can Teach Us About Economics (and Our Future)*. London: John Murray, 2019, p.197.
6   Dylan Jones, *iPod, Therefore I Am: A Personal Journey through Music*. London: Phoenix, 2005, p.19.

how insubstantial it was." [7] This indicates that although listening
behavior is breaking new ground, it leads into the cultural past. The
list becomes a container medium for one's own past, a form of auto-
biographical self-expression that can either be shared on the iTunes
Store, to be evaluated and downloaded by others, or that further
cements one's own taste through consumption. Abundance provokes
a nostalgia for a time of scarcity, even though the material is handled
playfully and re-combinatorially.

In 2011, music journalist Simon Reynolds looked back pessi-
mistically on the previous decade, stating that pop culture suffers
from *Retromania*—the title of his book—of which one symptom is
the "mash-up." The mash-up is a form of cultural production that
responds to the new reception experience by means of the playlist.
Thus, if the iPod's shuffle mode seamlessly transitions from Whitney
Houston's "I Wanna Dance with Somebody (Who Loves Me)" to
Cyndi Lauper's "Girls Just Want to Have Fun," why not combine the
two and call it "Girls Just Wanna Dance?" Reynolds laments that this
recombination of pop history leads to a flattening of differences. Lost
is the signature of the now time, the sound of the present. While technological devolution had made mixtaping possible, the technological
progress of the iPod had led to cultural devolution.

Beginning with the iTunes Store, the industry once more regains
its interpretative authority. The playlists it offers are arranged thematically according to the seasons or special occasions, such as Halloween,
or curated by companies that, unlike on the radio, make their pres-
ence felt through curatorial-creative services. While listeners dili-
gently compile and share playlists containing the soundtracks to their
lives, the industry once again finds a way to turn this new trend into
a profit. The sale of music as complete playlists on the iTunes Store
countered the trend of consumption becoming more targeted as a
result of increased unbundling as well as of the noticeable reduction
in the profit margins of the platforms, labels, and rights owners as a
result of the change in consumer behavior.

Therefore, it is no surprise when Apple soon after tries to provide more automated buying impulses using influence algorithms
already perfected by online marketplace Amazon. In 2008, a feature
called "Genius" is introduced, providing recommendations based

7   Ibid., p. 21.

on consumers' iTunes libraries. The charts, with their claim to completeness and interpretative authority over the understanding of popularity, are becoming less important; the trend is moving ever further towards personalization. This also involves increased monitoring and evaluation of data sets that are extracted from, at times, unsuspecting users.

The foundations for the datafication of download shops and streaming platforms had already been laid. Pandora Media implemented the Music Genome Project at the beginning of the decade in 2000, enabling a precise analysis of music according to certain parameters such as tempo, gender of the lead vocalist, and lead instrument. On the one hand, this resembles the so-called Smart Playlists iTunes had made available to its users, allowing them to generate automatic playlists from their libraries according to all kinds of parameters such as genre or even song length. Personalization qua categorization.

In his essay "Neo-Muzak and the Business of Mood," on the other hand, Paul Allen Anderson notes that the company Muzak used a very similar indexing of music for its programming of radio shows and as background music for the non-places of consumption.[8] The playlisting of Muzak is intended to stimulate the productivity of factory workers or generate a peaceful and friendly atmosphere in department stores. The desire for similar impacts increases with the success of streaming. The decisive factor here is a Swedish company, Spotify.

While Pandora initially follows a "lean-back method" recognizable from radio, Spotify is launched in 2008 as primarily a "lean forward" platform,[9] a "celestial jukebox" that listeners can browse at any time without restrictions.[10] The promise is twofold: Listeners

8   Paul Allen Anderson, "Neo-Muzak and the Business of Mood," *Critical Inquiry*, vol. 41, no 4 (2015), pp. 811–40, here p. 823.

9   Marc Hogan, "Up Next: How Playlists Are Curating the Future of Music," *Pitchfork* (July 16, 2015), https://pitchfork.com/features/article/9686 -up-next-how-playlists-are-curating-the-future-of-music/, accessed July 7, 2020.

10   The term was already coined in 1994 by Paul Goldstein and has been used in relation to Spotify and other streaming platforms before. See among others, Stephen Schultze, "Is Spotify the Celestial Jukebox for Music?," *Freedom to Tinker* (September 18, 2012), https://freedom -to-tinker.com/2012/09/18/is-spotify-the-celestial-jukebox-for-music/, accessed July 19, 2020.

are offered the prospect of discovering new music, and musicians the prospect of being discovered. Spotify offers playlist functions from the very beginning, but this feature does not come into focus until the end of 2012. The reason? Abundance. Although users are eager to create their own playlists and share them with each other, as on a social network, the platform quickly takes control of the practice.

This is because the abundance of digital space must be kept artificially scarce in order to facilitate consumption and increase the platform's added value. Like the iTunes Store before it, Spotify increasingly relies on editorially created playlists. In 2012, as the authors of *Spotify Teardown* put it: the company's strategy undergoes a "curatorial turn," which "meant that Spotify began to transform itself from being a simple *distributor* of music to the *producer* of a unique service."[11] The act of curation itself becomes a commodity, consumed by the user, while the playlist becomes a meta-commodity.

Again, technological progress leads to a form of cultural devolution. Following its acquisition of the music-intelligence company The Echo Nest in 2014, not long after Spotify launches the weekly "Discover Weekly" playlist, tailored to individuals' activities. The feature contributes significantly to the popularity of the platform, promising both personalization and convenience—a mixtape that does not need to be recorded, and which, in theory at least, strikes just the right chord week after week. The recommendation algorithms are fed from data sets that track user activity far beyond fixed parameters such as age or gender. At the same time, consumers perform a new form of digital labor by disclosing their behavior, which in turn is evaluated and thus provides the basis for new recommendations (and for advertising, of course). However, although this form of recommendation is personalized, it is not necessarily personal: People are made comparable as dynamic data sets and no longer lean over a heavenly jukebox. Instead, they lean back and become passive listeners. More appropriately, the promise of discovery inscribed in "Discover Weekly" should be understood as a form of nudging that is typical of surveillance capitalism.[12] This is no longer a case of

11   Ibid., n.p.
12   See among others, Anna-Verena Nosthoff and Felix Maschewski,
      Die Gesellschaft der Wearables. Digitale Verführung und soziale Kontrolle.
      Berlin: Nicolai Publishing & Intelligence, 2019, pp. 30–34.

ROCK & ROLL

"TEQUILA"
THE CHAMPS / SANTO & JOHNNY
"SLEEPWALK"

"EARTH ANGEL"
THE PENGUINS
"HEY SENORITA"

"O KNOW HIM IS TO LOVE HIM"
THE TEDDY BEARS / DONNY BROOKS
"MISSION BELL"

"BALLAD OF A TEENAGE QUE
JOHNNY CASH / ROY ORBISON
"OOBY DOOBY"

"A TEENAGER IN LOVE"
DION & THE BELMONTS / THE CLOVERS
"LOVE POTION #9"

"HOUND DOG"
ELVIS PRESLEY
"DON'T BE CRUEL"

"SHAKE, RATTLE & ROLL"
BILL HALEY & THE COMETS
"EE YOU LATER ALLIGATOR"

"ROCKIN' ROBIN"
BOBBY DAY / ERNIE FIELD
"IN THE MOOD"

"IT'S NOW OR NEVER"
ELVIS PRESLEY
"A MESS OF BLUES"

"GET A JOB"
THE SILHOUETTES
"I AM LONELY"

"leaning forward." The playlist establishes a form of gentle subordination to   the principles of order it defines.

Whether it is Apple Beats' focus on supposedly hand-picked celebrity playlists or Spotify tailoring its compilations to specific moments, feelings, and activities, playlists seize on the emotional cachet that lists have enjoyed since the triumph of the charts and, later on, of self-created mixtapes. The effects of "singularization" and "autonomy" praised by Hosokawa in "The Walkman Effect" thus make a return under different auspices.

The monopolistic celebrity system, which has always sustained the history of pop music, is strengthened and expanded. In addition to well-known musicians, even politicians like Barack Obama present their own playlists. This entails a shift in the attention economy away from the actual producers of music to the curators, further emphasizing that in the context of streaming, the commodity of music is subordinated to the meta-commodity of the playlist. At the same time, an atomization of the listeners takes place, who each week are confronted with a different, distinct playlist designed to reflect their own personal taste—or rather, to create it.

As with other upheavals, such as the introduction of the LP, music itself adapts to these conditions. LPs triggered the development of the album as an art form. In digital space, however, it becomes fragmented and the individual parts decontextualized—with at times paradoxical consequences. When Ed Sheeran released his album ÷ in 2017, all sixteen songs were in the top twenty of the British singles charts at the same time, because the audience not only listens to the LP in one go, but is presented with the different songs in individual playlists.[13] The release of Drake's album *Scorpion* is even more extreme: Following deals between Spotify and the relevant label, songs are prominently featured in lists that are completely unrelated, such as "Best of British." Apple even promotes *Scorpion* in conjunction with the language assistance app Siri.[14] The payola of the radio age has definitively returned, disguised as personalization through playlists or language assistance.

13   Laura Snapes, "Ed Sheeran has 16 songs in the Top 20—and it's a sign of how sick the charts are," the *Guardian* (March 10, 2017), https://www.theguardian.com/music/musicblog/2017/mar/10/ed-sheeran-has-16-songs-in-the-top-20-and-its-a-sign-of-how-sick-the-charts-are, accessed July 19, 2020.
14   Krueger, *Rockonomics*, p. 182.

Sometimes the production and publishing process already follows the dynamic logic of the playlist, as in the case of Kanye West. Some abandon the album format almost completely, instead relying on the steady release of individual tracks. The German rapper Capital Bra, for example, released a full four albums between 2016 and 2019, before starting to put out singles from 2018, some of which would later appear on albums but not all. On the one hand, this leaves fans with the task of compiling their personal "best-of" as a playlist, while, on the other hand, it triggers a devolution of the album into a compilation, which it had been before the success of the album-as-artwork that began in the 1960s.

Economic constraints thus increasingly set the tone, influencing songwriting, which becomes more and more attention seeking and provides, as songwriter Charlie Harding puts it, a kind of "executive summary" of what will follow during the first thirty seconds of the song.[15] Why? To make sure that no songs are skipped in the playlist environment (royalties only become payable after thirty seconds of playing time). It even creates its own sound: Similar to the mash-up phenomenon of the previous decade, the new form of reception gives rise to distinct aesthetic parameters. Like the charts before it, the playlist defines—from the standpoint of economics—what popularity actually means, what counts as popular, and what the corresponding music sounds like. In fact, it sounds just like "Spotify-Core," described by music journalist Liz Pelly as "muted, mid-tempo, melancholy pop, a sound that has practically become synonymous with the platform."[16] The playlist is not only the new commodity of streaming—it even creates its own sound. How can this be reconciled with personalization, with the active involvement of listeners?

Probably not at all. Even the dual promise of discovery and being discovered cannot be fulfilled. The design and consumption of playlists increasingly force artists to adapt to the new conditions, while playlists present their music to listeners without a lot of additional

15   Marc Hogan, "Uncovering How Streaming Is Changing the Sound of Pop," *Pitchfork* (September 25, 2017), https://pitchfork.com/features/article/uncovering-how-streaming-is-changing-the-sound-of-pop/, accessed July 19, 2020.

16   Liz Pelly, "Streambait Pop," *The Baffler* (December 11, 2018), https://thebaffler.com/downstream/streambait-pop-pelly, accessed July 19, 2020.

information. This is why streaming platforms are criticized for not, or at least not fully, providing the contextualization—artwork or liner notes—that physical products such as vinyl or CDs provide. This argument is not only reactionary—because it longs for old systems of order—but also not entirely correct. Playlists create their very own contexts for the audience by becoming instruments for (self-)optimization in the streaming environment, utilized for the regulation of emotional life as if they were a drug. The "Beast Mode" playlist as an upper to wake up in the morning, "Ambient Chill" as a downer to wind down after work. While the mixtape was seen as an expression of your personality, the playlist is now used to influence your mood.

With their playlists, platforms like Spotify do not satisfy a demand, but rather produce it in the first place, as Attali observed at the end of the 1970s vis-à-vis the culture industry in general. "Music is prophecy," he wrote in *Noise*, his book about the political economy of music, "its styles and economic organization are ahead of the rest of society because it explores, much faster than material reality can, the entire range of possibilities in a given code."[17] In the history of the playlist, music is dissolved in commodity form and at the same time reaggregated, fitted into a meta-commodity, which itself is constantly and dynamically changing, anticipating its own future from the past of its listeners. It separates its listeners by both homogenizing them as individuals and the cultural products they consume, thus continuing processes that were initiated long before its emergence. As form and medium, the playlist continues to grow in popularity among consumers whose behavior it registers and, as some fear, increasingly regulates. The playlist creates order over those who use it to experience music, to express, or improve themselves.

Translated from the German by Kevin Kennedy

17   Attali, *Noise*, p. 11.

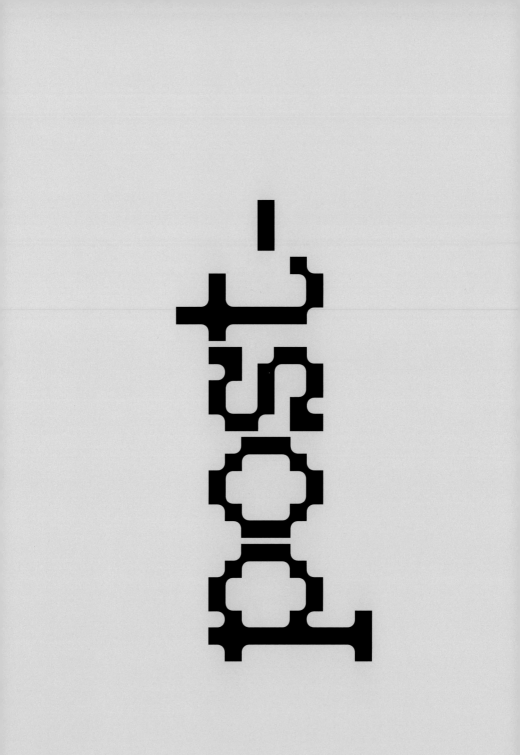

everyone

Playlists and the Datafication of Music Formatting
The Song and the Sequence

The song is the basic unit of popular music. Crafted by the song-writer, performed by the performer, curated by the DJ, and sold as a single—the song is the atom of the music universe. A hit single can break a new artist and become the soundtrack to an entire summer. It can capture a moment and evoke an era. This is precisely why it sounds so counterintuitive to claim the following: The music listening experience rarely centers on the song. Instead, the listening session is typically characterized by a particular arrangement of *songs*, a succession of tracks organized in various sequences. These sequences may take the form of an album played on a CD or record player, a countdown on a hits radio program, or an artist on shuffle on an MP3 player or streaming platform.[1] Even when we seek out a particular earworm to play on its own, we often do so on repeat.

It is not only our experience with music that is defined by sequence. In his classic study *Television: Technology and Cultural Form*, Raymond Williams recognized what he called "planned flow" to be "the defining characteristic of broadcasting."[2] For Williams, the real program is not the show but the schedule—the particular sequence of TV shows and commercials, designed around the purpose of capturing and retaining viewers. Williams' point seems prescient to anyone who has ever clicked on a YouTube video, only to find themselves hours later, wondering what happened to their evening.

But even when advertisers are not calling the shots, a similar dedication and attention to "planned flow" prevails. Since the 1960s, on both sides of the Atlantic, "serious" recording artists recorded LPs, and these "long play" albums assumed the symbolic capital of books. The Beach Boys' album *Pet Sounds*, released in 1966, has been described as the LP that "invented—and in some sense perfected—the idea that an album could be more than the sum of its parts."[3]

1   In this article, I use *form* or *format* to mean "the way in which something is arranged or set out" rather than in its more technical sense, such as "the MP3 format."

2   Raymond Williams, *Television: Technology and Cultural Form*. Hove: Psychology Press, 2003, p. 86.

Sequence mattered, as "the order of the tracks, not just the tracks themselves, could be laden with meaning."[4] Just as the novelist writes a novel comprised of sequentially arranged chapters, the musician writes an album made up of tracks that proceed to tell an aural story.

Of course, listeners were never obliged to listen to albums in the way artists intended. As Devon Powers points out, a whole host of "changer technologies" emerged in the latter decades of the twentieth century to facilitate both the randomized play of individual tracks and continuous play beyond the temporal limits of the album.[5] The digitalization of music, followed by the emergence in the early 2000s of MP3 players and the Apple iTunes Store, seemed to signal that the listener (in concert with the almighty shuffle feature) had won the battle over sequence. Today, as digital downloads have declined and music consumption has moved onto streaming platforms—such as Spotify and Apple Music in the West or Tencent Music and MelOn in the East—new modes of organizing and sequencing music have emerged. Particularly noteworthy is the rise to dominance of the streaming playlist.[6]

From Planned to Programmable Flow

While anyone can create their own playlist, streaming platforms heavily promote their own playlists over playlists compiled by users and other third parties. Unlike the traditional album, which is fixed upon release, platform-curated playlists can be made and remade infinitely. Unlike radio playlists, streaming playlists are programmable through datafied user feedback. This extends the malleability and modularity

3   Devon Powers, "Lost in the Shuffle: Technology, History, and the Idea of Musical Randomness," *Critical Studies in Media Communication*, vol. 31, no. 3 (2014), pp. 244–64, here p. 250.

4   Ibid.

5   Ibid., p. 251.

6   According to Spotify, playlist consumption accounts for approximately two-thirds of monthly content hours on the platform. See United States Securities and Exchange Commission, "Form F-1 Registration Statement, Spotify Technology, S.A." (2018), https://www.sec.gov/Archives/edgar/data/1639920/000119312518092759/d494294df1a.htm, accessed July 2, 2020.

of the music-listening experience, optimizing "planned flow" to increase engagement and to fit selected contexts, moods, or particular listener profiles.

Platform-curated playlists can be divided into two general categories: editorial and algorithmic. In practice, however, the popular "man-versus-machine" dichotomy breaks down. While editorial playlists like Spotify's "RapCaviar" are "handcrafted" by curators, decisions to add, replace, or change the position of a track on a playlist are strongly supported by data and proprietary software.[7] Spotify playlist curators employ a software tool with the acronym PUMA (Playlist Usage Monitoring and Analysis) to track "the overall performance of the playlist as a whole, with colorful charts and graphs illustrating listeners' age range, gender, geographical region, time of day, subscription tier, and more."[8] PUMA also monitors the number of plays, skips, and saves, and so on, of individual tracks on any playlist. Tracks can then be added or replaced based on these performance metrics. Likewise, before it was folded into YouTube Music, Google Play Music curators relied on a content management system called Jamza, which ranked individual tracks with a "Song Score"—a multipoint metric that aggregated average play length, number of skips, and number of "thumbs-ups." Jamza also helped curators by recommending songs for playlists based on ones that had already been chosen.[9]

As recounted in several journalistic interviews with playlist curators, the order of the tracks—the "planned flow" of an editorial playlist—is particularly important. "Position matters, completely. We are obsessive about it," a Spotify curator explains.[10] Likewise, an editor

7   Tiziano Bonini and Alessandro Gandini, "'First Week is Editorial, Second Week is Algorithmic': Platform Gatekeepers and the Platformization of Music Curation," *Social Media + Society*, vol. 5, no. 4 (2019), https://journals.sagepub.com/doi/epub/10.1177/2056305119880006, accessed September 14, 2020.

8   Reggie Ugwu, quoted from Liz Pelly, "Not All Spotify Playlists Are Created Equal," *cashmusic.org* (June 21, 2017), https://watt.cashmusic.org/writing/thesecretlivesofplaylists, accessed July 7, 2020.

9   Reggie Ugwu, "Inside the Playlist Factory," *BuzzFeed News* (July 13, 2016), https://www.buzzfeed.com/reggieugwu/the-unsung-heroes-of-the-music-streaming-boom?utm_term=.hvMKLQwaDz#.euAJyq9GEa, accessed September 14, 2020.

THE RECOMMENDER

Music and more to check out   **This week: Alan Donohoe, The Rakes**

WHAT I'M LISTENING TO RIGHT NOW

1 Jamie Lidell
Music Will Not Last
"This is my favourite on the album because it's most like his live show."

2 Bassomatic
Fascinating Rhythm
"It starts with a soul diva singing and kicks in with old-school piano-house."

3 Bloc Party
So Here We Are
"I'm into Bloc Party's slower stuff."

4 Amerie
1 Thing
"This is really sharp, catchy and bold."

5 J-Kwon
Tipsy
"The subject matter is about him getting drunk. I can relate to that."

6 Puccini
Humming Chorus from Madame Butterfly
"I'm not into opera really – I find it a bit irritating, not this one though."

7 Franz Ferdinand
Do You Want To
"They've exceeded themselves!"

8 David Bowie
Heroes
"We've tried to rip off this period of Bowie."

9 Rufus Wainwright
Oh What A World
"As philosophical as you can be in a song without going too Radiohead."

10 TTC
Dans Le Club
"French hip-hop so I don't understand the lyrics. I hope they aren't dodgy."

It's a wonderful world – just ask Louis Armstrong

MY FAVOURITE NEW BANDS

Lidell: an experimental supermarket where shop staff are shadows – but still the same great value!

Jamie Lidell
"After The Rakes, his is probably the best live show I've seen! I saw him play this drum'n'bass do with Squarepusher a while ago. I'd never heard of him before but as soon as he came on, he stole the show and since then I've tried to go and see him when I can. I guess I'd describe his sound as somewhere between techno and Motown. It's crazy but also pleasant on the ear. And it's definitely pushing things forward – it's not retro in any way which is refreshing. He's different live to on-the-record as he's always got loads of mind-blowing visuals going on."

The Go! Team
"I can hear Brighton in this – like I can imagine people into big beat getting into it. It's fresh-sounding and original. We've played with them a couple of times although in this case I prefer the album more than the live experience."

Giant Drag
"They're an American boy-girl duo – they played before us at CMJ in New York. The singer's got this great sense of humour. She did a cover of Chris Isaak's 'Wicked Game' and tried to convince everyone she'd written it."

MY BIGGEST INFLUENCE

Grolsch
"It helps us to make some decent tunes. I like to think it helps make our shows more fun too. I mean, we don't get completely trashed because then I wouldn't be able to remember any lyrics, but it definitely helps me dance onstage."

A GUILTY PLEASURE

Daniel Bedingfield
"Matthew [Rakes guitarist] was saying Jamie Lidell reminded him of Daniel so I put on an acoustic version of 'Gotta Get Thru This' to prove him wrong. Instead, I realised it had a good melody."

OTHER STUFF

FILM **Old School**
"I tried to rack my brains and think of something that changed my life but I couldn't, so I'll say this dumb, drunken college one with Snoop Dogg in."

BOOK **The Unbearable Lightness Of Being, by Milan Kundera**
"There are some bits that are gross where he's describing explicit sex, and other philosophical bits where he talks Nietzsche – a bit like our album."

DVD **The Office**
"We must be boring – we quote David Brent all the time. In the DVD you get to see Gareth in tight cycling shorts."

FANBOY — What if Franz's influences WEREN'T cool!?!

FISH FINGER SARNIES
My favourite food. I got the recipe from a Naked Chef cookbook. Jamie says to squash the sandwich a little to make it taste better – it just does. Pukka.

LENNY HENRY
Best. Comedian. Ever. Did you ever see that sketch where he plays a school girl? Changed my life.

JOHN MAJOR
Not so much his politics but more his state of mind. One word – STYLE.

LLEWELYN-BOWEN
His art. Not his TV work. It's underground. Bob's art teacher told him never to use gold or silver. Lawrence rips up the rule book. He lives his life by the leaf.

POLICE ACADEMY FILMS
Especially the later ones. We love watching them repeated on channel 5. That sound FX guy invented human beat-box!

beer beer, nee-naw

itsmountpleasant.com

at Deezer said of his work, "When creating playlists, I probably spend the most time on the order. You can have the right tracks in a playlist, but if they don't sound right next to each other—if you listen to it all and something jars—you'll lose people."[11]

This curation process is further automated with algorithmic playlists, such as Spotify's "Discover Weekly," "Daily Mix," and "Your Summer Rewind," all of which are personalized for individual streaming listeners. While streaming platforms protect the precise makeup of their algorithms as intellectual property—and while these algorithms are constantly tweaked and updated—it is possible to make some very general observations about how they operate. Drawing from an article published by Spotify software engineer Sophia Ciocca, it is clear that Spotify's algorithmically curated playlists rely on at least three different sources and methods of data analysis: collaborative filtering, natural language processing (NLP), and raw audio models.[12]

Collaborative filtering is a widely used technique across the web for comparing behavioral preferences and making recommendations. It is perhaps most visible on Amazon: "Customers who bought this item also bought...." On streaming platforms such as Spotify, collaborative filtering algorithms group similar users together. Users are deemed "similar" if they have listened to the same songs or if they have similar usage patterns around music. Collaborative filtering is then employed to recommend a song or artist to one user that the other user has listened to.

At the same time, NLP is used to build a mathematical representation of the textual associations between artists and songs. As Ciocca explains:

10   Ciara Allen, "I Create Spotify Playlists For A Living" [video], YouTube (posted by *BuzzFeed News*, July 11, 2017), https://www.youtube.com/watch?time_continue=29&v=Ji_WfHxatoQ&feature=emb_title, accessed September 14, 2020.

11   Stuart Dredge, "The New Tastemakers: A Day in the Life of a Music-Streaming Playlister," *The Guardian* (May 23, 2016), https://www.theguardian.com/technology/2016/may/23/music-streaming-services-playlister-sam-lee-deezer, accessed September 24, 2020.

12   Sophia Ciocca, "How Does Spotify Know You So Well?," *Medium* (October 10, 2017), https://medium.com/s/story/spotifys-discover-weekly-how-machine-learning-finds-your-new-music-19a41ab76efe, accessed July 18, 2020.

> Spotify crawls the web constantly looking for blog posts and other written text about music to figure out what people are saying about specific artists and songs—which adjectives and what particular language is frequently used in reference to those artists and songs, and which other artists and songs are also being discussed alongside them.[13]

This allows Spotify to map the cultural connections between songs and artists, finding similar artists and music based on what people are saying online.

However, to account for new or unpopular tracks that have little usage data—the so-called "cold-start problem"—Spotify employs "machine listening" on raw audio in order to identify songs with similar acoustic patterns. This involves convolutional neural networks, which is essentially facial recognition technology adapted for the analysis of audio data instead of pixels.[14] While it evaluates aspects such as the key, mode, and tempo of a track, this technology also measures more unconventional features such as "valence," "speechiness," and "danceability."[15] This involves translating the subjective language of music into the objective language of numbers. For example, in Spotify's application programming interface (API) documentation, "valence" is described as:

> A measure from 0.0 to 1.0 describing the musical positiveness conveyed by a track. Tracks with high valence sound more positive (e. g. happy, cheerful, euphoric), while tracks with low valence sound more negative (e. g. sad, depressed, angry).[16]

In short, algorithmic playlists are never the result of one algorithm: They involve numerous algorithms and methods of data analysis to

13   Ibid., n.p.
14   Ibid.
15   Asher Tobin Chodos, "What Does Music Mean to Spotify? An Essay on Musical Significance in the Era of Digital Curation,"INSAM *Journal of Contemporary Music, Art and Technology*, vol. 1, no. 2 (2019), pp. 36–64, here p. 49.
16   "Get Audio Features for a Track," Spotify for Developers, https://developer.spotify.com/documentation/web-api/reference/tracks/get-audio-features/, accessed July 18, 2020.

construct similarity. Spotify's signature algorithmic playlist "Discover Weekly"—a personally tailored playlist of thirty new tracks, delivered to each subscriber every Monday morning—is a good example of this kind of hybrid recommendation system that is built upon collaborative filtering, NLP, and machine listening.

Most listeners care little about these details, but these details are important. Every one of the small decisions that go into building the recommendation algorithm for a playlist like "Discover Weekly" has a real effect on which songs are heard, and in turn which artists are able to make a living from their music. For example, in building your personal weekly playlist, "Discover Weekly" gives more weight to tracks found on popular playlists and on those curated by Spotify.[17] Likewise, if a dance track does not meet Spotify's definition of "danceability," it may not be added to the "Dance Party" playlist. All this makes both Spotify and its streaming competitors powerful gatekeepers in the music world.

It is thus crucial to interrogate the assumptions that lay beneath such methods—assumptions about the listening subject and the (social) role of music. To start with, platforms such as Spotify understand the listener-subject in ways that recall the approach of behavioral psychologists to the study of the individual. Early behaviorists such as B. F. Skinner argued that the true object of psychology should be behavior rather than consciousness. Only behavior provides publicly observable data upon which to construct rigorous and scientifically sound models of how and why people do what they do.[18] In much the same way, streaming platforms are less interested in how users self-identify as music fans or even in demographic markers that traditionally acted as a proxy for music preferences. Instead, they take an epistemologically behaviorist position to understanding music taste. For example, in order to personalize recommendations and playlists, Spotify builds a "taste profile" for each user of its service. A taste profile is a dynamic record of one's musical identity,

17   Adam Pasick, "The Magic that Makes Spotify's Discover Weekly Playlists so Damn Good," *Quartz* (December 21, 2015), http://qz.com/571007/the-magic-that-makes-spotifys-discover-weekly-playlists-so-damn-good/, accessed July 18, 2020.

18   Jay Moore, "The Basic Principles of Behaviorism," in Bruce Thyer (ed.), *The Philosophical Legacy of Behaviorism.* Dordrecht: Springer, 1999, pp. 41–68.

generated primarily by implicit behavioral feedback. This feedback is collected every time we search for a song or an artist we like, listen to tracks, add songs to a playlist, or skip tracks. Such implicit feedback is much easier to collect on a large-scale basis than explicit feedback (where users actively rate content or describe their preferences), and it is also considered a better indicator of the music we actually listen to—rather than the music we would like to be associated with.

Streaming platforms also appear to promote an online version of neo-behaviorism through their approach to affecting and conditioning listening behavior. A basic proposition of behavioral psychology is that behavior occurs within an environment and that behavior can be manipulated by manipulating that environment. Driven by the goal of maximizing engagement, platforms utilize playlists as cybernetic laboratories. Tracks are continuously being added, replaced, and moved up and down a playlist based on performance metrics. A/B testing of playlist cover images and other features is ongoing. The playlist here serves as the environment, or a "container," which "functions as a stabilizing device that prepares music for mathematical calculation and transport optimization."[19] Like the famous "Skinner box"—used to study behavioral responses in lab animals—playlists provide a cage within which the "listener-rat" can be studied and optimal listening behavior can be induced.

This may sound somewhat hyperbolic. But as several scholars have pointed out, *listeners* are recast as *users* on streaming platforms; they "outsourc[e] the creation, maintenance, and storage of their music collections" to the platform.[20] In turn, the organization of music is modulated to fit particular user profiles and moments in order to induce engagement.

Here, we move from a theory of the streaming listener to the assumptions about the role of music that seem to underlie streaming platforms. In a fascinating experiment that monitored how Spotify Featured Playlists presented themselves to users in three different countries, Eriksson and Johansson concluded that "music was generally described as performative of motivation and energy":

19   Maria Eriksson, "The Editorial Playlist as Container Technology: On Spotify and the Logistical Role of Digital Music Packages," *Journal of Cultural Economy*, vol. 13, no. 4 (2020), pp. 415–27.

20   Jeremy Morris, *Selling Digital Music, Formatting Culture*. Berkeley, CA: University of California Press, 2015, p. 168.

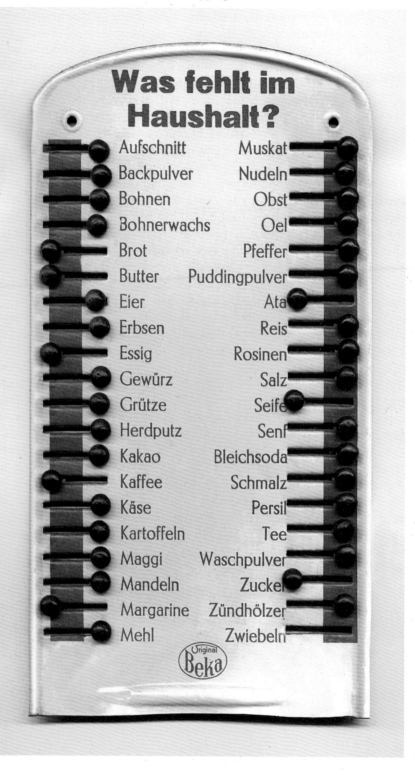

[W]e were repeatedly invited to view music consumption as an accompaniment to other, more significant tasks, rather than as an activity in its own right. The goal, here, was not only increased productivity but also a general improvement of one's mental state and attitude to life, something seen in play-list descriptions like, 'Get happy with this pick-me-up playlist full of feel good songs!,' 'stay focused and smart with these house tracks,' and 'Nothing hurts as heartbreak. These songs will help you have a good cry.'[21]

This signals a functionalist perspective that regards music as a back-ground accompaniment to everyday routines, an amplifier for expe-riences, and an enabler of moods. This point is most clearly high-lighted in Spotify's promise to "soundtrack your life." In an essay that explores what music "means" to Spotify, Asher Tobin Chodos explains how "the subtle creep of the 'soundtrack'" descriptor engen-ders the idea that "music is generally supplemental to other activities and modes of consumption."[22]

A glance at Spotify's top Featured Playlists reveals an abun-dance of contexts, like "Party," "Road Trip," and "Workout," and play-lists with titles such as "Summer BBQ" or "Songs to Sing in the Car." Also prominent are playlists that reference particular moods, such as "Happy Hits." While the foregrounding of context- and mood-based playlists over genre may seem like a banal design decision, the prin-ciple that underlies it can be traced all the way to the top brass at the company. "We're not in the music space," Spotify CEO Daniel Ek famously told *The New Yorker,* "we're in the moment space."[23] Much more than simply a rhetorical flourish, to be about "moments" is to be about serving not individual users but, rather, their "context states."[24]

Of course, music has always been "used" by listeners to struc-ture their lives and activities.[25] Streaming playlists are just the latest incarnation of the practice of turning to music to amplify and organize

21   Maria Eriksson and Anna Johansson, "'Keep Smiling!': Time, Functionality and Intimacy in Spotify's Featured Playlists," *Cultural Analysis,* vol. 16, no. 1 (2017), pp. 67–82, here p. 75.
22   Chodos, "What Does Music Mean to Spotify?," p. 46.
23   John Seabrook, "Is Spotify the Music Industry's Friend or its Foe?," *The New Yorker* (November 17, 2014), https://www.newyorker.com/magazine/2014/11/24/revenue-streams, accessed July 18, 2020.

our everyday experiences. However, as detailed above, datafied user feedback allows for the organization of music on streaming platforms to be modulated to fit particular user profiles and context moments. Since 2019, Spotify has been algorithmically personalizing some of its most popular editorial playlists, because "songs that one person may want to sing in the shower just might not make sense for everyone else."[26] This is likely only the beginning, as cutting-edge scientific research is exploring artificial-intelligence techniques that involve real-time learning and adaptation to sequential music preferences.[27] This has been made possible by the proliferation of mobile devices which permit the collection of data points on location, motion, time of day, and nearby contacts. Increasingly, instead of listeners "attending" to music, music (to borrow from the etymology of *attendere*) is literally made to "to stretch toward" its users.

Implications for Musicians

Research has confirmed the crucial importance of Spotify-curated playlists to the careers of musicians. A study by the European Commission determined that a track placement on Spotify's "Today's Top Hits" playlist resulted in up to US $163,000 in additional revenue. Other popular Spotify-curated playlists resulted in an even higher payout: "Viva Latino!" was found to generate between $303,047 and $424,265 in added revenue per track.[28] It is thus not surprising that musicians—and the record labels and managers that represent

24   Roberto Pagano et al., "The Contextual Turn: From Context-Aware to Context-Driven Recommender Systems," *RecSys '16: Proceedings of the 10th* ACM *Conference on Recommender Systems* (September 2016). New York: ACM, pp. 249–52.

25   Eric Drott, "Music in the Work of Social Reproduction," *Public Culture*, vol. 15, no. 2 (2019), pp. 162–83.

26   "Our Playlist Ecosystem Is Evolving: Here's What It Means for Artists & Their Teams," Spotify for Artists (March 26, 2019), https://artists.spotify .com/blog/our-playlist-ecosystem-is-evolving, accessed July 18, 2020.

27   Elad Liebman, Maytal Saar-Tsechansky, and Peter Stone, "The Right Music at the Right Time: Adaptive Personalized Playlists Based on Sequence Modeling," MIS *Quarterly*, vol. 43, no. 3 (2019), pp. 765–86.

28   Luis Aguiar and Joel Waldfogel, *Platforms, Promotion, and Product Discovery: Evidence from Spotify Playlists*. Cambridge, MA: National Bureau of Economic Research, 2018.

them—have focused all their attention in recent years on getting their tracks on the most popular playlists.

However, while the placement of a track on a popular playlist can result in a nice payday, artists are becoming increasingly concerned with the lack of engagement displayed by most playlist listeners.[29] Industry analyst Cherie Hu has pointed to a "growing attitude of disillusionment among up-and-coming artists and labels that playlists are not as meaningful to, or aligned with, their business as the hype had promised."[30] This is because artists recognize that playlists are there to serve the platform, not the artist. The platform needs to keep users engaged and this means creating products that are—to use the Silicon Valley jargon—"sticky." Playlists fulfill that purpose, but in doing so "the artist is disposable in service of the product."[31]

Indeed, Spotify's "Marquee"-sponsored playlists are far bigger than the artists or songs that appear on them. "RapCaviar," the world's biggest and most influential hip-hop playlist, is followed by over 13 million people across the globe. Not limited to being a platform-specific or online brand, this playlist has even had its own tour since 2017: the RapCaviar Live series.

Research conducted via interviews and focus groups with listeners has confirmed that it is the playlist that is being listened to, not its constituent songs. In focus groups conducted with streaming users in Moscow and Stockholm, it was found that playlist consumption was "leading away from knowledge about artists" as "the songs themselves were moved to the background within the fast-moving 'flow' of playlist music."[32] As one participant in the study expressed:

> [S]omeone starts playing their playlist and then you get hooked
> on something, and you ask what it is, but you often forget

---

29   Cherie Hu, "Millions of Followers? Yes, But Some Top Spotify Playlists Fall Short on Engagement," *Billboard* (July 3, 2018), https://www.billboard.com/articles/business/8463174/spotify-playlists-engagement-analysis-study, accessed July 18, 2020.

30   Cherie Hu, "Our New 'Post-Playlist' Reality," *Revue* Issue #41 (posted 2019), https://www.getrevue.co/profile/cheriehu42/issues/our-new-post-playlist-reality-138493, no longer available.

31   Ibid.

32   Sofia Johansson, Ann Werner, Patrik Åker, and Greg Goldenzwaig, *Streaming Music: Practices, Media, Cultures*. New York: Routledge, 2017, p. 49.

about what it was, or you forget to ask because there's another song, and another song, and then the song you wanted to ask about is, like, just number 10 on the list.[33]

To the extent that this quote can be seen as at all representative, this is worrisome for musicians.

By choosing how artists and tracks are grouped and ordered, the playlist creator (either in the form of a person or an algorithm) redefines the meaning of the music. Furthermore, just as the unbundling and re-bundling of news content by aggregators like Google News shifts power away from the newspaper editor, the disassembling of albums and their re-assembly as playlists shifts "curatorial power" away from the artist.[34] As a result, musicians have less control over the presentation of their work than they did in the album era. In place of the artist, the curator of the music experience—the platform—becomes the "creator." Format matters, therefore, not only for what it can tell us about transformations in the consumption of music, but also because it points to the shifting locus of curatorial power and in turn, who gets to be considered creative.

Alongside a particular theory of the listening subject, we can thus ascertain these platforms' understanding of both music and the musicians who support the playlist. While listeners are "users," music becomes "content,"[35] and musicians become "a production facility for playlists."[36] In turn, the playlist threatens to subsume the artist and her song—the musical foundation upon which everything else rests.

33 Ibid.
34 Robert Prey, "Locating Power in Platformization: Music Streaming Playlists and Curatorial Power," *Social Media + Society*, vol. 6, no. 2 (2020), https://doi.org/10.1177/2056305120933291, accessed September 14, 2020.
35 Keith Negus, "From Creator to Data: The Post-Record Music Industry and the Digital Conglomerates," *Media, Culture & Society*, vol. 41, no. 3 (2019), pp. 367–84.
36 Mark Mulligan, "Time to Stop Playing the Velocity Game," MIDiA *Research* (July 3, 2020), https://midiaresearch.com/blog/time-to-stop-playing-the-velocity-game?utm_source=MIDiA+Research+Newsletter&utm_campaign=4299b909fa-EMAIL_CAMPAIGN_2019_01_14_12_03_COPY_01&utm_medium=email&utm_term=0_8602b921cd-4299b909fa-523290919, accessed September 14, 2020.

What about the
Unplaylistable Artists?

Music streaming is a relatively new concept: Spotify launched in 2008, followed by Apple Music in 2015, and Amazon Music the following year. And yet, the very concept of music streaming services—the current sites of corporate absorption and flattening of music culture—has become quickly and deeply wedged within our cultural consciousness. It can feel like an inevitability, when in fact, it is not.

Looking at the effects of streaming on music is one way of understanding the homogenizing effects of platform capitalism on culture. In a fairly short space of time, streaming platforms have attempted to reshape how music is valued and contextualized en masse. One of the biggest factors has been the "playlistification" of music by these services, and the emergence of playlists based on moods, activities, and affects.

The rise of the playlist represents a grim evolution in the long history of corporate encroachment on music, and the entire playlist environment has consequences for artists and listeners alike. As the years have passed, a *playlist logic* that defines this moment has emerged. This is a logic that is incompatible with art and music, because it is one that prizes popularity and passivity as its most valued metrics. Playlists are embedded within the logic of capitalism. And the values of the streaming economy have become embedded in some music itself, creating a type of "platform culture" as opposed to music culture.

It is difficult to speak about the all-consuming consequences of these music and media shifts without specifically honing in on Spotify, despite Spotify being just one private company among the many major players in the music streaming space. There are several reasons for this. It is not that the company's competitors have not also adopted some of its tactics of mood playlisting in its wake—and they, too, must be held accountable for the effects of these new systems on artists and communities, among their other many egregious offenses. But Spotify is an appropriate place to start in unpacking the reach of playlist logic, not least because it has most aggressively set these new norms across the music industries. In part this is because Spotify is not a hardware company: The products it hypes to users and to Wall Street are its on-platform offerings—its music recommendations and personalized playlists. Spotify is also an advertising platform with a free tier, and this means that playlists contribute to the data it can use when segmenting audiences and attempting to sell its advertising inventory. The size of Spotify's user base, of course, is another reason for its outsized influence: It is the largest global music streaming service, and it seems to be on a ceaseless quest for domination of not just the music industries, but also podcast and radio listening—intent on capturing the whole of "audio."

Playlists Respond to the Market

In the early years of Spotify, the user was more in control of their listening experience. The main way of interacting with the interface was through the search bar, and so the listener would need to think about what it was they wanted to hear. As chronicled in the 2018 book *Spotify Teardown: Inside the Black Box of Streaming Music*, this all changed in 2013 when Spotify made a turn towards playlists, both personalized and curated. In their recounting of the ways Spotify has packaged and pushed music, the authors wrote that "the single most important change to Spotify was the so-called curatorial turn, in 2013, from a search-based interface focused on simply accessing music to its current emphasis on delivering crafted music recommendations."[1]

Particularly in the early years, streaming services went to great lengths to brand these playlists as merely an updated version of the mixtape. But there are aspects of how playlists are designed, promoted, and engaged with, which create a new paradigm. Firstly, they are heavy on music from major labels, which Spotify is contractually obligated to promote. In fact, the major labels even maintain their own third-party playlist brands on the platform, under profiles called Filtr (owned by Sony), Digster (owned by Universal), and Topsify (owned by Warner). The playlists made by major labels through these channels are given more prominence on the platform than other third-party curated playlists and are often promoted on the Spotify front page as "announcements" (when really they form part of the agreed advertising inventory).

1   Maria Eriksson, Rasmus Fleischer, Anna Johansson, et al., *Spotify Teardown: Inside the Black Box of Streaming Music*. Cambridge, MA: MIT Press, 2019, p. 117.

assembled

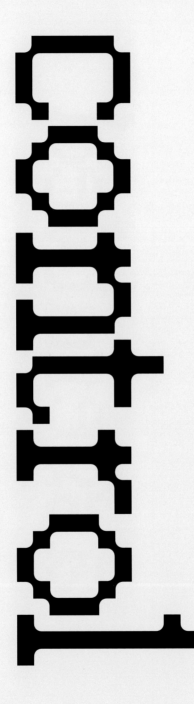

Another notable difference between streaming playlists and playlists or mixtapes that appear elsewhere on other platforms, is the sheer amount of data that is collected on users' day-to-day activities and how this is used to fine-tune these playlist offerings. Another way of looking at it, though, is that Spotify is constantly engaged in behavioral surveillance: always watching, capturing—each time you press play, skip, finish a song, every time you search, make a playlist—all of your activity.

Playlists, therefore, are not the fixed expressions of curatorial vision that streaming services like to paint them as. Whether programmed by an individual, a professional hired by a streaming company, or by a machine-learning algorithm, playlists are often designed to be refreshed regularly with decisions made by looking at data. In other words, playlists respond to the market. Their tracklists change with the ups and downs of "play counts"—the currency of the streaming economy.

The Tyranny of Popularity

The streaming environment being one of mass data collection also means that the failure or success of tracks, which fail, live, or die on the platform, is largely determined by abstract data. The songs that *stream well* are rewarded: they are added to more playlists by human curators; they are bumped algorithmically. The songs that *stream poorly* are removed or recommended with less frequency. All the while, the songs *streaming well* are often at an advantage to begin with because of major label contracts or big indie marketing budgets that get certain songs obligatory banner ads, premium platform promos, or playlist placements, all of which lead to more streams.

Over the years, countless artists and labels have spoken out about the flattening elements of this system: Songs that can be played over and over again in the background are the most highly rewarded. In a recent episode of Holly Herndon and Mat Dryhurst's podcast *Interdependence*, Herndon spoke to this dynamic, underlining the inherent absurdity of a system that treats *a song's ability to be played over and over again* as the ultimate form of value: "By accepting a per-play valuation of music, we accept that musical value is tied to music's ability to function in the background, and that's something that I categorically reject," Herndon said, explaining how she personally has been most affected by music that she does not necessarily listen to endlessly on repeat. Rather, the music that she has been the most impacted by is music that contains new and necessary ideas—like a good book or film. She continued:

> I think this will always be a fundamental flaw in the per-play model, and works to further marginalize music which has a different value metric at its core [...]. Easy to listen to music has historically been easier to monetize because it reaches more people, which is also fine, but that was balanced by people being able to spend 20, 30 dollars on an LP or CD to access music which didn't belong in the background.[2]

This requirement that music do well in the background, or do well on repeat in the background endlessly, is part of what comprises *playlist logic*—the guiding logic that makes a song *playlistable*.

"Playlist logic" is an extension of a dynamic that pervades our entire cultural landscape today: the tyranny of popularity. In the streaming world, streams beget streams beget streams; those streams beget more playlist placements and followers; more streams and playlist placements beget greater likelihood of tracks being algorithmically recommended. The flatter and less offensive something is, the more malleable to platform recontextualization—in the streaming world, that means its ability to sit alongside an advertisement for athleisure on a workout playlist *and* a liquor brand on a late-night party playlist—the more popular it becomes.

It all raises a key question: On commercial platforms, can culture viably exist beyond pop culture? Is it illogical or naive to even expect otherwise? Streaming services—as the centers of power in music, connected to Wall Street bottom lines—are inextricably entwined with the necessity of scaling. But scaling is not the objective of all artists, all types of music, or all music projects.

Playlists are useful to streaming services because, among other reasons, they facilitate audience segmentation, which makes selling advertising easier. And so, "playlist logic" fittingly values, above all

2   Holly Herndon and Mat Dryhurst, "Interdependence 5: Liz Pelly" [podcast 41:40 min.], *Interdependence* (June 17, 2020), https://interdependence.simplecast.com/episodes/interdependence-5-liz-pellynonpatronszv055d_C, accessed August 1, 2020.

else, what brands and advertising agencies call "engagement." Today's understanding of "engagement" is a particularly grim reimagining of that word, a mutation that has little to do with the actual meaning of the word. Instead, today, engagement merely means clicks. On streaming platforms, it means: How many plays did a track get? How many playlists was it added to? How many followers did it get?

The fallibility of using this kind of engagement as a way of determining the value of music is exposed by how quickly scamming and payola have infiltrated streaming services. Today, it only takes a quick Google search to turn up companies like Playlist Push, whose average campaign costs US $450 and claims access to over 970 curators and 23 million listeners, and Music Promotion Corp, which promises artists access to more than 2,000 Spotify Featured Playlists to promote their music. The latter promises to get artists onto the Official Spotify Chart, and offers packages starting at $10 for a single promotion, which will get the artist one playlist placement within three days.[3] Another package offered for $135, called "Spotify Viral," promises from 15,000 to 20,000 plays and monthly listeners within seven days.

Clearly, playlist logic ought to be called into question for several reasons, but one being that it is a logic that runs entirely on stats which are so easily manipulated by money, whether from scam artists or major labels. It is not so different from, say, scammers buying followers on Instagram—it is meaningless.

Passivity, Streambait, and Emotional Clichés

I have likened the resulting music and playlist trends to forms of neo-Muzak, a widespread dynamic of lean-back listening where streaming service users think less about which album or artist they are seeking out, and instead choose their music according to how they're feeling or how they want to feel. Today, the background listening of waiting rooms and elevators is all the more easily available for our headphones. In this environment, music serves the role of emotional regulation or perhaps just fills blank space in order to boost productivity.

3   Music Promotion Corp, "Spotify Promotion", https://www.music-promotioncorp.com/spotify-promotion/, accessed September 21, 2020.

One result of this shift has been the mass-scale decontextualization of music from its intended format (albums, EPs, or even just within the context of an artist's discography), with tracks instead recontextualized into packages that are more profitable for the streaming service. These tracks may be chosen simply for their ability to capture user attention—hooky enough to get a user to click "Play" in the first place, but inoffensive enough to keep said user from clicking away.

Because the music that is rewarded in this environment is often music that can fit within the parameters of baseline emotional clichés, like "chill" and "focus" and "happy" and "sad," another result has been a massive trend towards tracks dealing in emotional clichés in order to more easily fit into playlists dedicated to a specific emotion or affect. For a specific example, one need not look further than the artist Spotify has most championed for how intertwined his success has been with the platform—one who Spotify even wrote about in the forms the company filed when going public on the New York Stock Exchange. Lauv is an artist whose music seems designed specifically to fit within mood-and-affect playlists to the extent that his debut album, released in 2020, was titled simply ~*how i'm feeling*~. Scrolling below Lauv's albums on the platform, he offers repackaged "EPs" of the exact same songs that appear elsewhere in his catalogue, just rearranged with clickbait titles like "~*DRIVING VIBES*~," "~*PARTY VIBES*~," "~*LONELY*~," and "~*WORK OUT W LAUV*~."

Ultimately, much of playlist logic represents just a repackaging of the basic principles of advertising and marketing, a way of thinking about music that previously would have been reserved for the Lauvs of the world—the most commercial and mainstream artists and labels—but which now is a source of pressure for artists of all scopes.

One Million Spotify-Core Musicians Making a Living off their Art

A fairly common response to outlining the issues of playlist logic, mood playlisting, and streambait is: How is this different from easy listening radio? The logic of capitalism has always defined the mainstream music industry—it is *the music industry!* Plus, are there not music listeners who *want* to listen to music in this way?

Indeed, it is true that passive music listening existed before the streaming era. And to name a technological shift as the root cause

of the many issues defining the plight of musicians today would be a dramatic oversimplification. The point, instead, is the ways that these technologies have been adapted by the mainstream commercial music industry in order to more efficiently accomplish its monopolistic goals.

What is new here is the fact that musicians, labels, and listeners of all scopes and scales are currently being aggressively sold this model as a one-size-fits-all solution. Like other players in the platform and streaming economies, Spotify has built its brand on the idea of neutrality, of being an open marketplace where anyone can be heard. We are persuaded that this is a model for all artists and listeners, including artists who create vastly different types of music, have different motivations for making music, use different ways of connecting with audiences, and desire different ways of conducting business.

Through Spotify's artist-facing program, Spotify for Artists, it regularly publishes videos and blog posts teaching artists tips and tricks for navigating the platform and building their career on Spotify—reminding musicians that if they just hustle, study their artist data, and act accordingly, they too can pull themselves up the playlist ladder.

But, as we have seen, in actuality the playlist environment is one that routinely rewards and even incentivizes the same type of sounds: sounds that do well on mood playlists. But what about the artists whose music does not do well as background fodder? What about the unplaylistable artists?

In late July of 2020, Spotify's co-founder and CEO, Daniel Ek, did an interview with the website *Music Ally* that was met with widespread criticism from the music community: "Some artists that used to do well in the past may not do well in this future landscape, where you can't record music once every three to four years and think that's going to be enough," said Ek. "The artists today that are making it realise that it's about creating a continuous engagement with their fans. It is about putting the work in, about the storytelling around the album, and about keeping a continuous dialogue with your fans."[4]

4   Stuart Dredge, interview: "Spotify CEO Talks Covid-19, Artist Incomes and Podcasting," *Music Ally* (July 30, 2020), https://musically .com/2020/07/30/spotify-ceo-talks-covid-19-artist-incomes-and -podcasting-interview/, accessed August 1, 2020.

In other words, Ek is saying that there are types of musicians who *do well* on Spotify and certain artists who *do not do well* on Spotify—but what he failed to admit was the extent to which an artist's ability to make background music for mood playlist brands is key to *doing well* in this environment. This all makes clear what Ek really meant in 2018, when he mentioned his personal mission for "one million artists to be able to live off their art"[5] from Spotify—it seems that what he meant in fact was one million artists making streambait and behaving like influencer-type content-creators.

All Playlists are
Advertising Something

It should be noted here also how over the past decade, in addition to the playlists that are created by Spotify itself, the platform has also become a popular destination for influencers and advertisers looking to market their personal brands and products. Paid subscribers may not hear audio ads played intermittently between every few songs, but they are still subject to a significant amount of advertising. And even when playlists are not shilling for brands like Nike or Starbucks, playlists are still shilling: for Spotify and its playlists.

All playlists are Spotify products, which is an important distinction to make from a labor perspective. Spotify encourages its listeners to form habits around coming to the platform for its own products, not for artists or albums. When you type an artist's name into the search bar on Spotify, before the results show you songs and albums, it will show you the Spotify-branded playlists the artist appears on. For example, if you type in "Noname" you will be directed towards "This is No Name," "Noname Radio," "Mellow Bars," and "Free Form" before her own albums.

This has consequences for artists, especially independent artists or those whose principles might one day lead them to challenge Spotify about its practices, perhaps to try to hold it accountable for a greater level of transparency and fairness towards those who supply the work on which its platform is built. Say the artist threatens to remove their music if Spotify does not meet their demands; if listener habits are

5   Ibid.

WHAT GOES ON!

GIMME TEN! A lot

SELEKTOR

PLATTEN

Art Brut
Brilliant! Tragic!
Cooking Vinyl/Indigo
★★

einen erwachsenen Nenner zu bringen. Erst war sie von Klassik und dem Gedanken fasziniert, Opernsängerin zu werden. Später entdeckte sie Punk und Computersoftware. Daraus macht sie nun einen vollelektronischen Kältekammersound, der den von Cabaret Voltaire und Fever Ray ähnelt. Auf ihm kann sich Stelmanis mit ihrem kräftigen Organ nach Belieben ausbreiten. Vom Prinzip her funktionieren Austra nicht viel anders als etwa Zola Jesus.

Die
Redaktion
bewertet
Neuerscheinungen

Laura Ewert
Redakteurin

dj charts

MATTHIAS TANZMANN LEIPZIG, MOON HARBOUR
1. Shlomi Aber - Freakside
2. Marlow & Claudia Nehls - Water (Jackmate Remix)
3. Lazy Fat People - Pixelgirl (C2 Remix)
4. Pan-Pot - What Is What / Wake Up
5. Jackmate - Nomads
6. Stefan Goldmann - Aurora / Beluga
7. Marko Fürstenberg - Surphased EP
8. Seuil - Brune EP
9. Brendon Moeller - Jazz Space EP
10. Zip & Baby Ford - Glidin' Along The Riverbed

ADA KÖLN, AREAL
1. Zander VT - Dig Your Own Rave
2. Sid LeRock - Naked (DJ Koze Remix)
3. Partial Arts - Trauermusik
4. Metope - Braga
5. Geiger - Good Evening (Remixe)
6. Pawel - Aesthetics Of Resistance
7. Synclair - Run, Johnny Run
8. International Pony - Still So Much
9. André Kraml - Dirty Fingernails (Remixe)
10. Sascha Funke - Ey

MELON AMSTERDAM, RATIO?MUSIC
1. Manfriday Feat. Larry Levan - Real Love
2. Beat Pharmacy Feat. Mutabaruka - Wata
3. Broke - Overthat
4. Guy Gerber - Sea Of Sand (Patrick Zigon Remix)
5. Move D - Got Thing
6. Kerri Chandler - Computer Games EP
7. Scott Grooves - Journey Beats
8. No Theory - #2
9. San Proper & De Schepper - Proper's Family Part 03
10. Melon - It Happens Every Spring

THOMAS FEHLMANN BERLIN, OCEAN
1. Tony Allen - Ole (Moritz Von Oswe
2. 3 Chairs - No Drum Machine
3. Sound Stream - Love Jam
4. Napiheads - The Bah / I See Heav
5. Amp Fiddler - Ridin (Carl Craig Rem
6. Meteo - Memento
7. Gudrun Gut - Move Me (Burger-Voi
8. Rotating Assembly - Seasons Of My
9. Yellowtail Feat. Jenny Fuijita - Over
10. Theo Parrish - I Am These Roots

TIGA MONTREAL, TURBO RECORDINGS
1. Chromeo - Tenderoni (Proxy Remix)
2. Guy Gerber & Chaim - Myspace
3. Kaliber 11 - A1
4. Kolombo & Libby - Shot Snap
5. Tiga - You Gonna Want Me (Tocodisco Remix)
6. Passarella Death Squad - Blackout
7. Dahlbäck & Dahlbäck - UNTITLED 3
8. Chromeo - Fancy Footwork (Dim Remix)
9. Proxy - Decoy
10. Prins Thomas - Fehrara

RIPPERTON LAUSANNE, LAZY FAT PEOPLE
1. Sid Le Rock - Naked (DJ Koze Remix)
2. Sonje - Fusteration
3. Novox - Marbles
4. Daso - La fée verte
5. Minz - Un/Mute EP
6. TG - Rhythm Acupuncture (Buttrich Remix)
7. John Daly - Sky dive EP
8. Pantha Du Prince - Asha
9. Lee Van Dowski - The Last Bounce (Ripperton Remix)
10. Sascha Funke - Auf Aix

DOMINIK EULBERG BONN, TRAUM/TRAPEZ
1. Clark - Ted
2. Plastik - Plastik
3. Gui Boratto - Beautiful Life
4. Riley Reinhold - Light In My Eyes
5. Gabriel Ananda - Trommelstunde
6. Quenum & Dachshund - Platzhirsch 11
7. Jason Emsley - Platzhirsch 13
8. Laven & MSO - Looking For Uhm Uhm
9. CH-Signal Laboratories - Hypnotica Scale 1
10. Stephan Bodzin - Planet Ypsilon

RUEDE HAGELSTEIN BERLIN, FREUND
1. Stefan Goldmann - Aurora / Beluga
2. Hot Chip - No Fit State (Audion Rer
3. Mr. White - The Sun Can't Compar
4. Benno Blome - Braitbend Noodles
5. Depeche Mode - Personal Jesus (Tr
6. Depeche Mode - The Sinner In Me (R
7. Douglas Greed - Girlfriend In A Co
8. Riton - Hammer Of Thor
9. Phage - Vut & Vat EP
10. Ruede Hagelstein - Sweaty Balls (

SERAFIN ZÜRICH, MOUNTAIN PEOPLE
1. Marko Fürstenberg - Surphased EP
2. Razzo - No.3
3. Britz - Mi Paris Rojo
4. Dan Curtin - Shadow Locked
5. Kerri Chandler - Computer Games EP
6. The Horn - The Rural Sea Part Two
7. Homero G- Deep Cut Collective 1
8. Re.3 - Fall Of Justice
9. Journey Man DJ's - Shelley's
10. John Thomas - Basic Voice Remix

SMOOTH PILOTS LEIPZIG, RESOUL RECORDS
1. Mari Boine - Vool Me (Henrik Schwarz Remix)
2. Escort - All That She Is
3. 40 Thieves - Ding Dong Moment
4. Good Guy Mikesh - Hol (G.G.Mikesh+Filburt Remix)
5. Makossa & Megablast Feat. Capitol A - Like A Rocket
6. Blackjoy - Untitled (Stefan Goldmann Marco Version)
7. Jennifer Cardini & Shonky - August in Paris
8. Tiger Stripes - Sun Watcher
9. Manoo - Kodjo
10. Martin Landsky - Let Me Dance (Seba K Remix)

D'JULZ PARIS, POKER FLAT / POUSSEZ LIGHT!
1. Shlomi Aber - Freak Side (Acid Mix)
2. TG - Rhythm Acupuncture (Martin Buttrich Remix)
3. Stefan Goldmann - Aurora
4. Aril Brikha - Akira
5. Luna City Express - Para Siempre
6. The Viewers - Black Images (Lazy Fat People Remix)
7. Kerri Chandler - Space Invader
8. GummiHz - Iaslos
9. QAnxx - Be Quiet (D'Julz Remix)
10. D'Julz - Flick It

SHONKY PARIS, FREAK'N'CHIC / MOBILEE
1. Iron Klock - Lazslawa
2. Decoy Lirazott - Gomil Shin
3. Marc Aritona - XTension
4. Boris Werner - Matchmaker
5. Cabonne - Smiling Papers
6. Jitzu - Idiot Savant
7. From Karaoke To Stardom - Loopish Opossum
8. Tim Xavier - Podium 3
9. Tom Clark - Service Station Remixes
10. Tiefschwarz - Ghost Track (Shonky Remix)

THOMAS FEHLMANN (continued)

MR. TIES BERLIN, THE MCF
1. Bostar Maniac - Bell Sweat Hell
2. Franco Cinelli - Antennia 2
3. Kaliber 70 - B1
4. Dirk Diggler - Grooviton (DopzyX Remix)
5. Billy D' Alessandro - Their Trick She Knows
6. The Exile Missfits - Sidewinder
7. Michel Dabay - Cat Fight
8. Adonis - We're Rocking Down The House
9. Datius - Poetry (The Year 2000 Remix)
10. Jorge Savoretti & Dario Zenker - The Joints Kinks

ALEXKID PARIS, FCOM
1. Robert Babicz - Sin (Ripperton Remix)
2. Jitzu - Glizzy Tank
3. Swero N Feat Nik Felice - Black Oun
4. Agnes - Hu Munda
5. Bukkobor & Fishbeck - Poltreabend
6. Mark Henning - Ring Of Fire
7. Jamie Jones - I Like You
8. Alexkid - Love Letters (M. Romboy and T. Paris Remixes)
9. Marco Resmann - Gavouche
10. Redkhope - Coffee And Cigarettes

SHINEDOE AMSTERDAM, INTACTO
1. Polder - Strong Ways
2. Will Saul & Tom Cooper - Sequential Circus
3. Marco Resman - Watercolour
4. Matei Di - Bortubbatiolo Spa
5. Remute - Cool But Strange (2000 And One Remix)
6. DJ Madskillz & Gregor Salto - Pecan Remix
7. Sasse - Gravity (Peter Dildo Remix)
8. Onur Özer - Red Cabaret
9. Unknown - White
10. John Thomas - Discotones

HENRIK SCHWARZ BERLIN, SUNDAY MUSIC
1. Wahoo - Get A Girl
2. Christian Frömmer - Strings Of Life
3. Freestyle Man - This Side Of The Moog
4. Ame - Balandine
5. Junior Boys - Like A Child (Carl Craig Remix)
6. Ahmad Jamal Trio - Wave
7. Joanna Mac Gregor - Heath On The Heather
8. X-Press 2 - Kill 100 (Lost Heroes Remix)
9. Holden - Lump
10. Henrik Schwarz - Walk Music

TOM CLARK BERLIN, HIGHGRADE
1. Paul Rich - Winter Ceremony
2. Audion - Death Is Nothing To Fear
3. Paco Osuna - Crazy
4. Todd Bodine - Spring EP
5. Format: B - Bronson Road
6. Tobias - Dici
7. Greg Cray - The Line
8. SLG - Sapot
9. Einzelt 23 - Thelen EP
10. Jorge Savoretti & Qrk - Wheel Of Time

AUDIO SOUL PROJECT CHICAGO, DESSOUS
1. Marc Romboy vs. Tyree Cooper - Lost
2. Alex Parsons - Storymore / Disco Drums
3. Audio Soul Project - Enter the Night
4. Choios - C Factor (Audio Soul Project Remix)
5. Alexkid & Chloe - Altenhirster Reblastered
6. Tommy Four Seven - Smoke
7. Tom Cooper - Goldrush
8. Physique - Closer Groove
9. FEX - Death or Glory
10. Redmouth - Anymore

AXEL BARTSCH KÖLN, SPORTCLUB / KOMPAKT
1. Trentemøller - Moon Dub
2. Axel Bartsch - In The Country
3. Faze Action - In The Trees (Carl Craig Remix)
4. Asem Shama - Being Franco Zoger
5. Axel Bartsch - Radio Controlled
6. Danilo Vigorito - Chastity
7. Pär Grindvik - Casa
8. Axel Bartsch - Easy
9. Matt Star - Hypno
10. Neal White & Meta - Bobsie

DAVE DK BERLIN, MOODMUSIC / PLAYHOUSE
1. Stefan Goldmann - Aurora
2. Sascha Funke - I Love This Tent
3. Seba K & Metro - Transit
4. Greg Oreck - The Line (Dub)
5. Dirt Crew - Deep We Are (House Version)
6. Funk D'Void & Phil Kieran - White Light
7. Aril Brikha - To Begin
8. Lopazz - Shore My Rhythm (Isolée Remix)
9. Eyerer & Chopstick - Haunting (Sleeper Thief Remix)
10. Lazy Fat People - Pixelgirl (Carl Craig Remix)

EUROKAI HAMBURG, LIEBE*DETAIL
1. Junior Boys - Like A Child (Carl Craig Remix)
2. Nick Höppner - Violet
3. Sebbo - Beirut Boogie
4. H.O.S.H - Steppenwolf
5. Gabriel Ananda - Trommelstunde
6. Junior Boys - Like A Child
7. Eldemis - Stately Yes
8. Atios - Time & Space
9. Pan-Pot - What Is What
10. Matthias Tanzmann - Nip Slip

MARTIN EYERER STUTTGART, TRAPEZ
1. Dusty Kid - Cowboys
2. Shlomi Aber - Freakside
3. David Squillace - Numash
4. Björn Willos - What If
5. Client - Drive (Eyerer & Namiko Remix)
6. Rich & Collins - Fortana
7. James What - Follicle
8. Stefan Goldmann - Beluga
9. Stewart Walker - Foreshadowing
10. Martin Eyerer & Oliver Klein - Tiflis

BREAKFASTCLUB LEIPZIG, DUSTED DECKS
1. Tolee - Impressed
2. Goose - Bring It Jon (Boris Dlugosch Remix)
3. Markus Lange - Shooting Tigers
4. Teenage Bad Girl - Cacotte (Boys Noize Remix)
5. Chopstick - Haunting
6. Rainer Weichold - Infinite Template (Kissy Sell Out Rem
7. Concept Original - The Pigeon Dancer
8. Boz le Belgium - La Musique
9. Moderate - Move Your Body

fully developed around going to playlists, what does it matter? They can just add something else to "Mellow Bars."

The playlist environment is therefore one that ultimately disempowers and devalues artists. This must be kept in mind when considering the extent to which Spotify is actively trying to develop fan cultures around some of its playlist brands.

One example is the massive promotional campaign for its so-called genre-less playlist "Pollen," launched in September of 2018. "Pollen" is a somewhat unusual playlist in the Spotify universe. The playlist environment by and large consists of increasingly niche categories: things like "Chill Vibes," "Instrumental Study," "Confidence Boost," or "Hanging Out Relaxing." But "Pollen" is none of these. Instead, it positions itself as a sort of authoritative playlist for people who do not want authoritative playlists to tell them what to listen to! "Pollen" is all marketing, built upon the immense resources that Spotify seems to have dispensed off-platform to build its playlist's "brand identity." Despite all the work that has gone into developing its reputation—its tagline is "Genre-less. Quality First."—it is actually a pretty aesthetically consistent slow-tempo blend of chill R&B, hip-hop, and indie pop. It currently has over 1.3 million followers.

As the designer who was hired to "brand" the playlist explains on the design studio's website:

> Moving away from traditional playlists that target one specific genre or mood, Pollen instead assembles an overall 'vibe' more akin to a lifestyle; a collection of moments rather than a singular category.[6]

The website lists a masthead of sorts, detailing twenty different individuals and entities who were involved in the development of the "Pollen" playlist, including a visual artist who was commissioned to draw portraits of musicians included on the playlist (in keeping with the "design system" of "Pollen") and floral designers who were hired to create elaborate bouquets that were sent to the playlist's cover artists as part of its promotion.

6   Porto Rocha, "Pollen", https://portorocha.com/pollen, accessed September 21, 2020.

In an interview, one Spotify playlist curator told *Complex* that playlists like "Pollen" are the platform's attempt to "contextualize around user communities, like what type of music are younger audiences ready for based on their other habits? What types of apps are they using, how are they engaging with our platform?"[7]

It seems as though these are playlists that attempt to incorporate the "streaming intelligence" which Spotify claims to use to segment audiences for its advertising clients, except here the advertising client is Spotify itself. If the very idea for the playlist is built around targeting a specific segment of its audience, then Spotify can all the more easily advertise to this base—whether by trying to sell ads to brands, or just advertising its own products. It doesn't need to draw listeners in and then try to define them for advertisers. It has already defined the audience and built the product around them.

Democratizing Exploitation

One independent artist, who spoke anonymously, reflected on their own experience working with an established indie label and the pressures the label put on them to keep up a regularly updated playlist. As the artist explained, the label was "pretty relaxed" about what they needed the artist to do promotion-wise:

> But one thing they mentioned at almost every meeting where
> we discussed album promotion was that they needed me
> to make a Spotify playlist of songs I liked and update it every
> Friday. I found it kind of strange how that was one of the
> main things they were pressuring me to do. And I suspect that
> their Spotify rep told them it would be beneficial for their
> artists to do this, and if they did this, there would be a higher
> chance [the label] would get put on Spotify editorial playlists.
> Because it was almost treated like a non-negotiable thing.

The artist continued:

7   Jacob Moore, "What is Lorem? Inside One of Spotify's Best New Playlists,"
     Complex (December 11, 2019), https://www.complex.com/pigeons
     -and-planes/2019/12/lorem-spotify-playlist, accessed August 1, 2020.

After that experience I got into the habit of continuing to update my playlist semi-regularly. But I'd catch myself feeling guilty. Sometimes I'd be putting it together and skipping a friend's song and, realizing that Spotify is keeping track of skip rates, wondering if they'll be penalized. And I think about how on Spotify's editorial playlists, getting placed near the top is a great honor because you get more plays [...]. It's hard to make something on that platform without being infected by the feeling of being surveilled.

Streaming services are obsessed with the narrative that they have democratized the music industries, but in reality what they have democratized is music industry exploitation: Now even you, the budding bedroom pop experimenter can be exploited by the same tools as the stars. The alleged "openness" of the new music economy conveys a false narrative of empowerment for the artist and fan alike. Anyone can release music, they say. Anyone can find fans. Fans discover the new music more than ever before. But these systems are managed entirely by the corporate class and industry elite, by major labels and brands. They determine what we see/hear, who wins and who loses, and the logic by which the system operates.

Because of its current all-consuming scale and the enormous financial interests wrapped up within it, streaming has been firmly established as the new norm, a flawed system that artists, writers, and listeners alike all struggle with. At present, the music world seems to be stuck in a cycle of reckoning, some acknowledging that perhaps our best way forward is to abandon this system entirely to carve out new modes of online music distribution that are not as exploitative of artists and listeners alike.

In 2020, a critical mass of enthusiasm against the streaming status quo has coalesced. The past couple of years have seen new waves of artists broadening the political and economic scope under which the issues of music streaming are understood. Artists have begun to imagine alternative projects as well as collectively organizing efforts to push back. Even when it comes to curating lists of music recommendations outside the limitations of playlist logic, there are projects like Avalon Emerson's Buy Music Club, a simple website that allows music fans to assemble playlists made from Bandcamp links, thereby encouraging them to buy the music if they like it. As the music-streaming critical newsletter *Penny Fractions* described it, Buy Music Club "helps offer a minor shift in how artists can position themselves within a post-streaming world."[8]

Much has been written about the effects of music streaming on artists, but we should also remember that playlist logic encourages a less meaningful, watered-down relationship with music for the listener, and this in itself is a disservice. The playlist listener can easily become trapped in a feedback loop of convenience and seamlessness, as their taste is surveilled, repackaged, and sold back to them, with streambait titles exploiting their base-level emotions. Most music fans would agree that there is something missing from this relationship.

If playlist logic recommodifies music in order to create value for streaming services, then countering playlist logic involves appreciating the material realities of music and the labor that creates it. An anti-playlist logic already exists, and has existed, but we'd benefit presently from remembering what comprises it: active listening, buying albums, supporting the community ecosystems that surround interdependent music, contributing to processes that properly contextualize music, and, most importantly, remembering that a post-streaming music world is possible.

8   David Turner, "Penny Fractions: A Half-Step Towards a Better Music Ecosystem," *Penny Fractions* (April 17, 2019), https://www.getrevue .com/profile/pennyfractions/issues/penny-fractions-a-half-step-towards -a-better-music-ecosystem-172439?utm_campaign=Penny%20 Fractions&utm_medium=email&utm_source=Revue%20newsletter, accessed August 1, 2020.

Listening Back

Maria Eriksson: Your work highlights the hidden nature of online surveillance in very hands-on and sometimes sonically beautiful ways. Did your interest in online surveillance grow out of your artistic practice as a musician?

Jasmine Guffond: It started during my Sound Studies Master's at the Universität der Künste (UdK, University of the Arts), Berlin. We were invited to collaborate on a Soundwalk with the Deutsche Staatsoper (German State Opera) on the theme of protest as it related to a history of protest around and within the opera building in Charlottenburg. At that time, I was reading in the news about how in New York directly after the Occupy movement protests CCTV cameras with facial recognition capabilities were installed. I subsequently discovered that protests in Germany are frequently videoed by the police, and that they have the capacity to cross-match the videos with ID databases or drivers' licenses using facial recognition technology (FRT).[1] It is also illegal in Germany to cover your face at a protest. One's right to be anonymous at protests is obviously being challenged, and I thought it would be interesting to explore a contemporary technological aspect of protest culture.

FRT is a particularly insidious form of biometric surveillance, because unlike iris scans or fingerprinting where you have to actively offer your finger or directly look into a camera, you don't have to actively do anything for FRT to identify you. As passive identification by FRT is possible, it is considered a "silent" technology. I wanted to give FRT algorithms a sound, to make them audible.[2] While researching for this project, I began reading surveillance studies articles and became increasingly interested in and appalled by contemporary digital surveillance.

1   Peter Ullrich and Gina Rosa Wollinger, "A Surveillance Studies Perspective on Protest Policing: The Case of Video Surveillance of Demonstrations in Germany," *Video Surveillance*, vol. 3, no. 1 (2011), pp. 12–38, here p. 27.
2   Jasmine Guffond, 2 Sonic Portraits: Your Individual Imprint," as part of *Das Grosse Buh, Protesten auf der Spur: Ein Soundwalk*, 2014, http://jasmineguffond.com/art/Sonic+Portraits+Deutsche+Oper, accessed July 15, 2020.

ME: Then the next project you worked on was *Listening Back*?

> JG: Actually, there was another project in between called
> *Anywhere, All The Time, A Permanent Soundtrack to Your Life.*[3]
> This is an app for Android devices that sonifies Wi-Fi and GPS
> networks, allowing users to walk around and hear the extent to
> which they can be tracked by ubiquitous and pervasive wireless
> infrastructures. I conducted listening walks with this project.
> By providing a direct sensory experience of the network data, I
> wanted to explore how it feels to live in a culture where our public
> and private space is being mediated by technological infrastruc-
> ture that has the capacity to empower via communication and
> yet compromise via mass surveillance. After this project, I began
> working on *Listening Back*, a web browser add-on that sonifies
> Internet cookies in real time.

ME: In the *Listening Back* project, you co-compose sonic patterns
together with the hidden monitoring systems that patrol the Web.
What is it like to make sounds in collaboration with cookies? How
would you describe the distribution of agency between yourself and
the tracking technologies you interact with in the *Listening Back*
plug-in? Do you think a cookie can be inspiring? Stimulating?

> JG: I'm inspired to produce an audible presence for otherwise
> intangible, yet ubiquitous and ever-effecting surveillance tech-
> nologies. Sound, similar to algorithmic surveillance processes,
> is not fixed in form, but rather constantly unfolding in multi-
> farious ways, and it is therefore ideal to represent the real-time
> online surveillance continuum. As a composition, the sonic out-
> put, particularly the structure, is determined by the cookie activ-
> ity generated by the user's web browsing. Another determining
> factor is the cookie data set I'm given access to via the Firefox
> and Chrome browser application programming interface (API),
> that is, what information Google and Mozilla provide to third-
> party developers. This is limited to each time a cookie gets sent

3   Jasmine Guffond, "Anywhere All the Time, A Permanent Soundtrack to
      Your Life," Android application/listening walk, 2015, http://jasmineguffond
      .com/art/Anywhere+All+The+Time, accessed July 14, 2020.

via the web server to the user's computer, deleted from the user's computer, or updated. However, the number of times a cookie is read by the browser and web server is not accessible via the API. What I found insightful was the extent to which certain technical processes can be hidden even from tech-savvy programmers, and how these processes of online-data extraction are in fact well-kept business secrets. In this sense, Google, Mozilla, and the data broker industry are my co-composers. This reflects a lack of user- as much as programmer agency in online environments where often by default we are opted-in to being tracked. It also highlights the ways in which major tech platforms and lesser-known data brokers are co-composing our online experience through the extraction, collection, aggregation, and sale of personal data, and then how it's used to curate our news feeds, access to information, and cultural experience.

ME: Was it difficult to find the right balance for how interruptive *Listening Back* should be?

JG: That's an interesting question, because this is a tricky balance to strike: to interrupt an otherwise seamless browsing experience, yet not completely disrupt that routine activity. It is important to draw attention to data-capture processes while the user is browsing the Web, because for an experiential insight into its prevalence and consistency it is crucial that algorithmic surveillance is experienced in situ. Sound is uniquely appropriate for this task, since we can listen peripherally, that is, while engaging in other activities such as checking emails, social media, shopping online, and so on.

To highlight the predominant networks of surveillance, I designed specific sound-signatures for the main tech corporations such as Google, Amazon, YouTube, and a flight search engine, since in general they are particularly "cookie active." During the development process, I also discovered that the Google analytics cookie is the most commonly used cookie across the entire World Wide Web and on our personal computers. For Facebook, I created a unique sound for the Like button, as well as for some of the regularly occurring third-party cookies implemented by less well-known data brokers. All the other

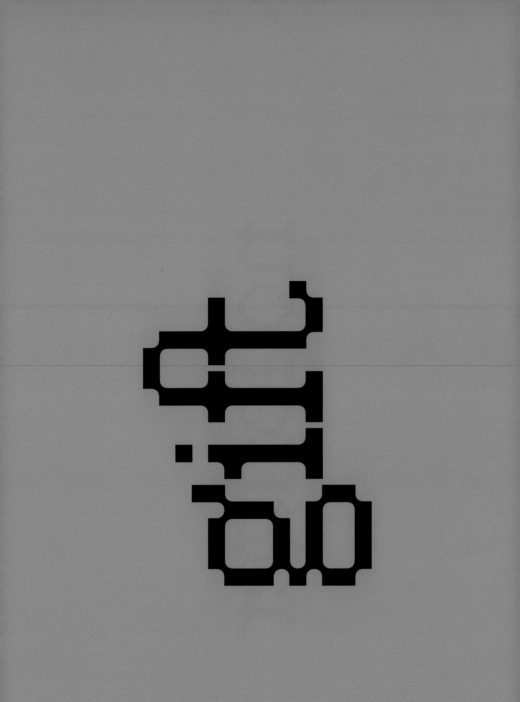

no longer

cookies—and there are so many—have a generic sound. This sound is somewhat reminiscent of a single guitar string being plucked, and as such, I felt it was suitable to being played continuously over time by numerous cookies.

ME: The add-on also allows users to personally adjust and tweak the sound of online trackers. Why was it important for you to include this feature?

JG: The *Listening Back* add-on was developed for anyone to install via the Chrome and Firefox stores,[4] as well as for live performances. The interface was designed primarily to allow performers to change the key, the octave, and the volume of individual cookies. Users can also adjust the volume of first- and third-party cookies. Third-party cookies are typically non-essential to the functioning of the Web and are usually inserted onto our computers by the data broker industry. Since many websites insert the same third-party cookies onto our computers, they are an effective way of tracking us across different websites. What becomes immediately apparent when listening to these data sets is that the principal ongoing sounds are generated by third-party cookies. Normally, first-party cookies are only present when loading a page. I think it is important to hear this distinction and understand that it is possible to navigate the Web without third-party cookies. All browsers offer the option to block third-party cookies, but this off button is hidden under layers of sub-menus. This is why the interface includes instructions under "how to block third-party cookies in the browser settings."

ME: The *Listening Back* add-on got me thinking about Shintaro Miyazaki's Algorhythmics project, which, among other things, sonifies and explores the rhythm of network traffic. Miyazaki writes about early computer history and describes how the practice of listening to machines was an integral part of computer engineering in the 1960s.[5]

4   The browser extensions can be found on: Chrome, https://chrome.google .com/webstore/detail/listening-back/gdkmphlncmoloepkpifnhneogc liiiah, accessed January 10, 2020; and Firefox, https://addons.mozilla.org /en-GB/firefox/addon/listening-back/, accessed January 10, 2020.

For instance, early mainframe computers (such as UNIVAC I, and the PASCAL computer developed by Philips Electronics) were complemented by auditory interfaces that allowed engineers to investigate the machine's workings via sound. As Miyazaki explains, these auditory interfaces were essentially amplifier–speaker systems that made the mechanical movements and processes of computers audible. Would you agree that your work could be described as a return to these early techniques of "hearing one's way" to the workings of computer machines? And if so, what do you see as the greatest potential benefit of (re)discovering computers through sound?

> JG: I am interested in the potential of sound to engage with political questions and, specifically, what it means for the study of online surveillance to engage sound with processes of understanding, representation, meaning, and knowledge production. Western societies are primarily ocular-centrist, so to listen is to engage a radically alternative perspective that invites the potential for new and alternate positions and understandings of phenomena and situations. Unlike these examples of listening to computers, where pre-existing sounds have been amplified, I'm utilizing sound referentially to draw aesthetic attention to specific tracking technologies that are otherwise inaudible. In this way, the sonification of real-time data processing is a methodology for engaging contemporary socio-technical and political situations by producing experiential spaces in which to listen and feel, and to reflect upon—in the case of *Listening Back*—the ways in which algorithmic surveillance intersects with our daily browsing experience. There is a hope that by audibly exposing data with political consequences, motivation for a new attentiveness, understanding, knowledge, and even change would be encouraged. By providing the opportunity to listen back to some of the data-capture processes that underlie our Web experience, I situate sound and listening as tactical mediums deployed as a counterforce to the asymmetric power dynamics inherent to online surveillance cultures.

5   Shintaro Miyazaki, "Algorhythmics: Understanding Micro-Temporality in Computational Cultures," *Computational Culture*, vol. 2 (28 September 2012), http://computationalculture.net/algorhythmics-understanding -micro-temporality-in-computational-cultures/.

ME: Why do you think that the faculty of vision has come to dominate our interaction with computers? And what do we stand to lose by not using our ears in the critical interrogation of digital technologies?

> JG: It's true that our engagement with the World Wide Web is mediated largely through screen devices and thereby predominantly, though not exclusively, through the visual sense. In the case of the *Listening Back* add-on, an audible presence is created to represent data capture processes that remain otherwise hidden beneath the screen or the graphical interface of the web browser. Sound in this context interrupts the visual surface of the Web and challenges what is apparent. This enables us to listen to questionable presumptions and re-examine comprehensions about the nature of everyday Web browsing.

ME: Tell me about your recent work on YouTube's Content ID system.

> JG: I was invited by HKW to do a lecture performance in 2019. The copyright directive had been passed in the European Parliament that year, and there was a lot of concern about Article 17 (formerly known as Article 13) which holds websites with user-submitted content responsible for copyright infringement. In practice, websites will need to introduce an upload filter that automatically checks uploaded content—that is, every tweet, post, shared photo, or video—for potential copyright infringement. European nations have two years in which to comply, so it was not entirely clear what the implications of algorithmically policing the Web in the EU would be. However, there is a precursor, which is YouTube's Content ID management system, an automated content-matching system that crossmatches uploaded videos with a database of copyrighted material. Recognition technology is incapable of understanding context, such as when copyright material is being used for satirical or educational purposes, which comes under fair-use agreements, and therefore isn't infringing copyright legislation. So, we have a system of algorithmic governing that has produced numerous, often hilarious, but ultimately concerning "false-positives." During the lecture performance, I uploaded remixes of false-positive videos I had collected from YouTube

Part II.

OVERTURE ... "Fra Diavolo" ... ... *Auber.*
Mr. WALTER HASTINGS.

BALLAD ... ... "The Heart bow'd down" ... ... *Balfe.*
Mr. JOSEPH KEENAN.

SONGS ... { "The Detective," "Don't take an old Man's Daughter," and "The Scamp, or They can't hold a candle to me." }
By THE FAMOUS ACTOR AND VOCALIST

MR. G. H. MACDERMOTT.

SONG ... ... "Love's Request." ... ... *Reichart.*
Mr. LACEY.

SONG ... "She wore a Wreath of Roses" ... *Knight.*
Madame LEIGH.

COMIC SONG ... "The Frenchman." ... ...
Mr. STUART.

SONG ... ... "The Village Blacksmith" ... ... *Weiss.*
Mr. JOHN EVANS.

MR. SMITH ALEXANDER (THE PREMIER VENTRILOQUIST),
Will then introduce his Wonderful and Amusing Entertainment.

PART SONG ... "Let the Hills Resound" ... *B. Richards.*
THE WILTON SQUARE CHOIR.

There will be an interval of 15 minutes between Parts 1 and 2, when the Band of the 2ND LONDON RIFLES will play a Selection of Popular Music.

to challenge its Content ID algorithm and to see how it would react to false-positive false-positives.

ME: What would you say should be our biggest concern with filtering technologies?

JG: Article 17 of the copyright directive is an example of how we are increasingly giving over agency to algorithms even though they are incapable of understanding something crucial, such as context. These automated systems are sometimes misunderstood as being neutral, unbiased, or imbued with a trustworthy logic, because they are a science or a technology. But this is clearly not the case.

ME: We have seen a rapid proliferation of digital tracking and surveillance technologies in 2020 ever since the coronavirus crisis started to unfold. What are your biggest fears and hopes when it comes to the future of the Internet and, in particular, our ways of accessing music online?

JG: Personally, I find it completely disturbing when widespread biometric surveillance infrastructures are hurriedly implemented during a crisis. I think we need to ask why governments are turning to Silicon Valley and tech corporations for solutions to a health pandemic. My fears extend beyond the Internet into every aspect of our lives—from contact tracing, education, and smart cities to turning on the lights, selecting music to listen to, and so on—being mediated, influenced, and controlled by technology that is largely produced by a few major tech corporations. The way we consume and access music is an aspect of this culture, as your Spotify research exposes. What I am referring to is how the business model for a major music-listening platform such as Spotify is based on the extraction and sale of personal data, which in turn is used to further influence our music consumption and even daily moods. Also, the Spotify interface—which is our point of contact with the platform and how we access music—guides how we listen and what we listen to. In this way, we become its subjects. Considering that Spotify is a business primarily concerned with advertising revenue, what does it mean exactly for it to be able to navigate and curate our access to and experience of music?

I often hear the corona virus crisis being referred to as a moment in which capitalism has been temporarily suspended, and while that is partly true—many industries have slowed down or paused—corporations such as Amazon and Zoom have profited hugely. At the root of online mass surveillance is a logic of extraction and accumulation, a logic that is shared with neoliberal capitalism and which directly contributes to the degradation of the environment and social and racial injustice and inequality. If I am to feel hopeful, then I'm radically hopeful for a transition into post-capitalist societies. One thing the pandemic has exemplified is that capitalism does not work in a crisis; rather, social welfare does.

+ Lina Brion is advisor to the Program Officer of the Academy of Arts, Berlin. Until September 2020 she was project coordinator in the Department of Music and Performing Arts at Haus der Kulturen der Welt, where she curated, among other things, the discourse programs for the music festivals. Brion studied cultural studies and philosophy in Berlin and Paris. She is co-editor (with Detlef Diederichsen) of *100 Jahre Copyright* (2019) in the series *Bibliothek 100 Gegenwart*.

+ Detlef Diederichsen has been head of the Department of Music and Performing Arts at Haus der Kulturen der Welt since 2006, where he has initiated several series and festivals, including *Wassermusik*, *On Music*, and *Worldtronics*, as well as theme days, such as *Unhuman Music (Unmenschliche Musik)*, *Doofe Musik*, *No! Music*, and *100 Jahre Copyright*. He previously worked as a musician, music producer, critic, journalist, editor, and translator. Since 1980, he has released several records with his band Die Zimmermänner, most recently the album *Ein Hund namens Arbeit*.

+   **Kristoffer Cornils** is a freelance cultural journalist and former editor at *Groove* and *Spex*. He works in Berlin and even sometimes lives there.

+   **Maria Eriksson** is a media scholar who studies the history and politics of everyday digital technologies at Humlab, Umeå University, Sweden. Her research is located at the intersection of software studies, media archaeology, social anthropology, and science and technology studies and centers on the interplay between culture and technology. Since May 2019, she has been a visiting lecturer at the Department of Arts, Media, and Philosophy at the University of Basel in Switzerland.

+   **Jasmine Guffond** is an artist and composer working at the interface of social, political, and technical infrastructures. Focused on electronic composition across music and art contexts, her practice spans live performance, recording, installation, and custom-made browser add-ons. Guffond has exhibited internationally, and her latest album, *Microphone Permission*, debuted on Editions Mego in March 2020.

+   **Liz Pelly** is a writer and critic based in New York. She is a contributing editor and columnist at *The Baffler*.

+   **Robert Prey** is a Canadian media scholar who studies the relationship between technology, capitalism, and culture at the University of Groningen in the Netherlands. His research and writings focus on algorithmic recommendation systems and the interdependent processes of "datafication" and "platformization." Prey's current focus is on music streaming platforms and the music, musicians, and industries developing around them.

Colophon

Das Neue Alphabet (The New Alphabet) is a publication series
by HKW (Haus der Kulturen der Welt).

The series is part of the HKW project *Das Neue Alphabet*
(2019–2022), supported by the Federal Government
Commissioner for Culture and the Media due to a ruling
of the German Bundestag.

Series Editors: Detlef Diederichsen, Anselm Franke,
        Katrin Klingan, Daniel Neugebauer, Bernd Scherer
Project Management: Philipp Albers
Managing Editor: Martin Hager
Copy-Editing: Mandi Gomez, Hannah Sarid de Mowbray
Design Concept: Olaf Nicolai with Malin Gewinner and
        Hannes Drißner

Vol. 2: *Listen to Lists*
Editors: Lina Brion, Detlef Diederichsen
Coordination: Lina Brion
Photo Editor: Christian Jungeblodt
Contributors: Kristoffer Cornils, Maria Eriksson,
        Jasmine Guffond, Liz Pelly, Robert Prey
Translations: Kevin Kennedy
Graphic Design: Malin Gewinner, Hannes Drißner,
        Markus Dreßen
Type-Setting: Hannah Witte
Fonts: FK Raster (Florian Karsten), Suisse BP Int'l (Ian Party),
        Lyon Text (Kai Bernau)
Image Editing: Scan Color Reprostudio GmbH, Leipzig
Printing and Binding: Gutenberg Beuys Feindruckerei GmbH,
        Langenhagen

Published by:
Spector Books
Harkortstr. 10
01407 Leipzig
www.spectorbooks.com

Distribution:
Germany, Austria: GVA Gemeinsame Verlagsauslieferung
    Göttingen GmbH & Co. KG, www.gva-verlage.de
Switzerland: AVA Verlagsauslieferung AG, www.ava.ch
France, Belgium: Interart Paris, www.interart.fr
UK: Central Books Ltd, www.centralbooks.com
USA, Canada, Central and South America, Africa:
    ARTBOOK | D.A.P. www.artbook.com
Japan: twelvebooks, www.twelve-books.com
South Korea: The Book Society, www.thebooksociety.org
Australia, New Zealand: Perimeter Distribution,
    www.perimeterdistribution.com

Haus der Kulturen der Welt
John-Foster-Dulles-Allee 10
D-10557 Berlin
www.hkw.de

Haus der Kulturen der Welt

**Haus der Kulturen der Welt is a business division of Kultur-
veranstaltungen des Bundes in Berlin GmbH (KBB).**

Director: Bernd Scherer
Managing Director: Charlotte Sieben
**Chairwoman of the Supervisory Board: Federal
    Government Commissioner for Culture
    and the Media Prof. Monika Grütters MdB**

Haus der Kulturen der Welt is supported by

Minister of State
for Culture and the Media

Federal Foreign Office

First Edition
Printed in Germany
ISBN: 978-3-95905-455-3

Recently published:
Vol. 1: *The New Alphabet*
Vol. 2: *Listen to Lists*
Vol. 3: *Counter_Readings of the Body*

Forthcoming:
Vol. 4: *Echo* (February 2021)
Vol. 5: *Skin and Code* (March 2021)
Vol. 6: *Carrier Bag Fiction* (April 2021)

Vol. 3:	*Counter_Readings of the Body*
Editor:	Daniel Neugebauer
Text:	Olympia Bukkakis, María do Mar Castro Varela, Rain Demetri, Sabine Mohamed, Bonaventure Soh Bejeng Ndikung, Olave Nduwanje, Jules Sturm, Julius Thissen
ISBN:	978-3-95905-459-1
	January 2021

When the human gaze falls on a body, it constructs and deconstructs it. The setting for this is our daily life in all its different shapes and forms. The human body functions here as a semiotic system, an archive, a fiction, a projection screen, or an alphabet. The gaze that encounters it may manifest as an antagonist—be it incisive or flawed—yet it can itself disappear from view. The texts and images brought together in this volume seek to remove the body from the firing line and away from these judging and derogatory glances. They act as mirrors redirecting looks, points of view, and ideas to enable us to understand implicit and explicit processes of reading.

Vol. 4:	*Echo*
Editors:	Nick Houde, Katrin Klingan, Johanna Schindler
Text:	Lisa Baraitser, Louis Chude-Sokei, Maya Indira Ganesh, Wesley Goatley, Xavier Le Roy, Luciana Parisi, Sascha Pohflepp, Sophia Roosth, Gary Thomlinson
ISBN:	978-3-95905-457-7
	February 2021

"If sound is birth and silence death, the echo trailing into infinity can only be the experience of life, the source of narrative and a pattern for history." Drawing on Louis Chude-Sokei's metaphorical, political, and technopoetic investigations, this volume experiments with how the echo of past ideas of life and form has brought forth the technologies and lifestyles that our contemporary world is based on. The essays, conversations, and artist contributions delineate a variegated array of technologies, creating an image of their past and their future potentials.

Vol. 5:   *Skin and Code*
Editor: Daniel Neugebauer
Contrib.:   Alyk Blue, Luce deLire, i-Päd, Rhea Ramjohn,
            Julia Velkova & Anne Kaun
ISBN: 978-3-95905-461-4
            March 2021

Just as physical violence leaves its marks on the skin, concep-
tual violence is written into interfaces via algorithms—in the
form of biases turned into pixels, as discrimination implanted
in memes in secret chat groups. The coding and decoding of
body surfaces and interfaces is contingent on a whole host of
norms. Yet these are not fixed: rather, they combine to create
a matrix of tastes, cultural influences, technical conditions,
and physical possibilities. The essays in this volume produce
an interdisciplinary noise between surface structures and
a selection of cavities: surfaces, skins, and interfaces are in-
jured, gauged, altered, or remedied.

Vol. 6:   *Carrier Bag Fiction*
Editors: Sarah Shin, Mathias Zeiske
Contrib.:   Federico Campagna, Dorothee Elmiger,
            Ursula K. Le Guin, Enis Maci a. o.
ISBN: 978-3-95905-463-8
            April 2021

What if humanity's primary inventions were not the Hero's spear
but rather a basket of wild oats, a medicine bundle, a story.
Ursula K. Le Guin's 1986 essay *The Carrier Bag Theory of Fiction*
presents a feminist story of technology that centres on the
collective sustenance of life, and reimagines the carrier bag as
a tool for telling strangely realistic fictions. New writings and
images respond to Le Guin's narrative practice of world-making
through gathering and holding.